James Moloney was a teacher in a number of government schools before becoming a teacher librarian. In 1983, he was appointed as teacher librarian for the junior school at Marist College Ashgrove, a boys' school in Brisbane where, as he says, he met every kind of boy reader, from the desperately keen to the intractably reluctant.

His interest in getting boys to read led him to have a go at writing himself, and in 1992 his first novel, *Crossfire*, was published. *Dougy, Gracey* and *Angela*, his acclaimed trilogy of novels, are widely read in high schools around the country. Now a full-time writer, he has more than a dozen books in print for children and young adults. His novels *A Bridge to Wiseman's Cove* and *Swashbuckler* both won the Children's Book Council of Australia's Book of the Year Award, and many of his other titles have won or been shortlisted for major awards.

James and his wife, Kate, have two daughters and a son, all of whom read avidly (though two took a nudge to get started).

boys
and
books

JAMES MOLONEY

boys and books

Building a culture of reading around our boys

with illustrations by
Cathy Wilcox

ABC
BOOKS

Published by ABC Books for the
AUSTRALIAN BROADCASTING CORPORATION
GPO Box 9994 Sydney NSW 2001

First published 2000

National Library of Australia
Cataloguing-in-Publication entry
Moloney, James, 1954–.
    Boys and books : building a culture of reading around
    our boys
    ISBN 0 7333 0846 5.
    1. Boys – Books and reading – Australia. 2. Sex
    differences in education – Australia. 3. Literacy –
    Australia. I. Wilcox, Cathy, 1963–. II. Title.
028.550994

Designed by Monkeyfish
Set in 12/16 Bembo by Asset Typesetting Pty Ltd, Sydney
Colour separations by Finsbury, Adelaide
Printed and bound in Australia by
Griffin Press, Adelaide

5 4 3 2 1

Contents

Acknowledgments

Many people have helped in the creation of this book.

I would like to thank Margaret Wild and Ali Lavau at ABC Books for inviting me to expand some earlier articles I had written into a longer work, and then seeing the project through with me.

As always, my wife Kate has given me wonderful support both personally and through her experience as teacher, librarian and mother.

The recommended reading lists which appear at the end of this book were compiled from a wide range of sources. However, these six friends and colleagues deserve a special mention:

Sue Richmond, teacher librarian and bookseller
Kerry Neary, teacher librarian at Corinda State
    High School
Rayma Turton, editor of *Magpies*
Helen Reynolds, teacher librarian at
    The Southport School
Jeff Shippey, teacher librarian at Slade Point
    State School
Lesley Reece, director of the Fremantle
    Children's Literature Centre

Agnes Nieuwenhuizen, Jane Connolly and Leonie Tyle lent me either their books or their ears along the way. Finally, I would like to thank the many dozens of subscribers of the OZTL-Net Bulletin Board who responded to my request for recommended books that work with boys.

Building a culture of reading around our boys

Boys are beautiful!

So says my friend and fellow writer, Glyn Parry. We need people like Glyn to remind us of this occasionally. After all, boys can be rowdy when we seek calm, morose when we want to know what ails them, and a hulking, even intimidating presence in a crowded house — they can be impossible. But, equally, boys can be tender and affectionate, and uncommonly generous with their time and energy — they can be a smiling, cheerful presence we would not be without. Yes, boys are beautiful.

But in recent years, a new mantra has been heard. Boys are in trouble. Drugs, violence and crime are mentioned, pointing towards an alienation from society that begs our scrutiny. But that is only a few boys, surely. Most boys are doing okay ... aren't they? This unsettling notion that more boys than we realise may be in trouble extends to our schools, where the comparative performance of boys and girls has become a popular topic for newspaper columnists. Unfortunately, much of the commentary has been concerned with sensational headlines such as 'Girls take 65 of top 100 places in VCE!', as though this is somehow against the natural order. Reading such headlines, I am disappointed that we do not seem to have moved beyond a 'battle of the sexes' mentality. Putting such narrow attitudes aside, is there really cause for concern?

When the figures are examined more closely, across all year levels and all ability groups, the true gender differences become clear. Among the higher and slightly above-average achievers, boys continue to hold their own, and in subjects traditionally thought of as 'male' — such as maths, science and computing — boys even retain a slight edge. The real concern lies with that large mass of average and below-average achievers. Here, girls clearly outperform their brothers. In particular, the reports tell us, boys struggle with literacy. Even the high achievers rarely list English as their favourite subject. I believe that these boys struggle because they do not live within a culture of reading.

This book is designed to show how parents and other interested adults can go about building a culture of reading around our boys. It starts by acknowledging that we have a problem which can be stated very simply. Among Australian boys, there is a widely reported reluctance to read. Our boys are not alone in this. The same phenomenon has been reported in Britain, North America and elsewhere. If this were of no greater concern to boys (and to those who love them) than a reluctance to eat broccoli, there would be no need to examine the problem or offer solutions. But a reluctance to read and the poor literacy skills associated with it have far-reaching effects on the lives of our boys, on the men they become, and on the society they influence. At a stage in human history now calling itself the 'information age', this is a worrying development.

The early chapters of this book first outline why reading is essential for our boys, and then examine why they seem so reluctant to read. The assumptions we have always made about this reluctance — boys are active, boys are busy etc. — are no longer enough. Recent research has given us a much clearer understanding of what holds our boys back from books and the reading habit. As with any conundrum, once the causes are understood, solutions begin to present themselves, and so later chapters are concerned with what parents and carers might do to defeat this reluctance.

Other writers have devised ways of encouraging children and teenagers to read, and some of their ideas are relevant here. But these earlier books have taken a broader view, looking at both boys and girls together. As a result, problems and solutions specific to boys have not been canvassed in any depth. I believe that there are difficulties arising from the culture of boys which do not apply to girls — difficulties that are becoming more pronounced rather than less with the passing of the years. It is time these were identified and challenged with a view to counteracting them.

Writers keen to encourage good reading habits have

also tended to remain within conventionally accepted boundaries when recommending reading material for our children. I have taken a different tack. In my opinion, issues of literary quality matter less than the need to get our boys reading willingly, well and often. This belief stems largely from fifteen years' experience as the librarian in an all-boys school. It comes also from a personal experience which is probably unfamiliar to those who have previously written about boys, books and reading — as a boy, I was reluctant to read myself. I know what it is like to prefer a game to a book, to read so slowly that getting through a novel becomes an exercise in frustration, and to despair of anyone ever writing a book that I wanted to read and that I *could* read.

I do not subscribe to theories which claim that the difficulties boys may be facing, both in school and out, have been brought about by feminism or the feminisation of our institutions. No, I believe that the problems are peculiarly masculine. At the same time, if we steadfastly refuse to accept boys as we find them, we will not get far in changing behaviours such as a reluctance to read. Such intransigence can hinder rather than help any reconstruction of masculinity to better meet the needs of our time. Consequently, an important section of this book is titled 'Reaching out to boys'. Whether a boy or a man, the person who embraces reading is more open to change than the person who disdains it.

A culture of reading is best grown from the seed, rather than grafted onto already existing habits, so parents with young sons will find much to consider in the chapters dealing with the years before school and the first three years of school itself. But if you have picked up this book hoping to turn around the reading reluctance of a boy already well into primary school or even secondary, there are practical suggestions for you to consider as well. Even if you do not see a substantial change in reading habits in the short term, establishing a clear framework around your son — where books are available, valued and discussed, and where good reading habits are modelled — may well make the difference to your son's adult life many years hence.

Both a boy's mother and his father have crucial roles to play in creating a culture of reading in the home and around their son. One of the final chapters is actually addressed to fathers, for, as this book explains in some detail, the attitudes and example of the significant men in a boy's life form much of this culture. For the majority of boys, their father is the most important role model — even during the adolescent years, when it may not appear so.

One thing I hope this book shows is that a society in which males do not read is a lesser society, not only for its men, but for its women as well. Whether man or woman, parent, teacher or librarian, whether caring for an infant or a teenager, we must all keep our eye on the ultimate prize — a thriving culture of reading among boys.

PART ONE

Boys and reading

CHAPTER ONE

Why boys need books and reading

We probably all agree that boys need books and reading — even if we haven't consciously thought through the reasons why. However, if your boy is reluctant to read, trying to turn him into an enthusiastic reader can seem an impossible task. You might even consider the effort you have already made to be more trouble than it is worth. But think about this. The relationship between a reluctance to read and poor literacy skills is like that of the chicken and the egg. Which is the cause and which the effect? They are inextricably entwined. Improve one and you will improve the other. Ignore one and the other will suffer as well. So a reluctance to read is not something we can afford to ignore, because if that reluctance is not challenged, a boy's literacy skills may either fail to develop in the first place, or may slip back from adequate to poor as he grows older.

Poor literacy skills — and the reluctance to read which goes hand-in-hand with them — can be disastrous for a boy's schooling and subsequent employment prospects — and, perhaps more importantly, his chances of leading a rich and fulfilling life.

School performance

In recent years, the federal government has instituted nationwide testing of the literacy and numeracy skills of children in Years 3 and 5. The figures below come from the National School English Survey, 1996.

This table shows the results for reading.

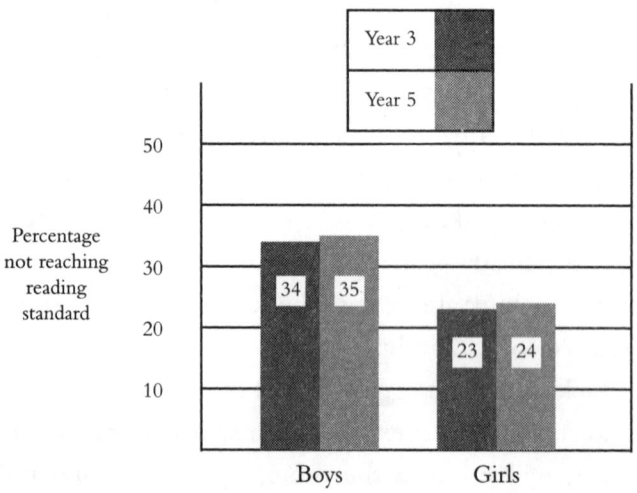

The results show that, overall, one third of boys have not learned to read adequately in the first three years of schooling. What is more, the figure for Year 5 was actually worse. Testing in the UK, the USA and Canada has produced similar results.

Following the performance of boys through into secondary school shows that, far from catching up as they mature, the gap between girls and boys widens as boys fall further behind. The most accurate predictor of poor academic performance in high school is below-average literacy levels in primary school. Few boys with reading problems seem able to improve their reading competence once they leave primary school. The dysfunction often extends beyond a boy's academic record as well. Weak literacy skills from an early age are also a predictor of behavioural problems in high school. These behavioural problems are often sheeted home to the frustration that accompanies continual academic failure in the many subjects where poor literacy skills leave the boys floundering.

English is a compulsory subject and a basic pre-requisite to further study. There are few subjects where poor literacy skills can be hidden or are considered unimportant. In fact, the ability to read underpins nearly all school subject areas. Boys who view Physical Education as an opportunity to escape the requirement of literacy often suffer a rude shock. Girls now regularly outperform boys in P.E.

It seems the only subject favoured by boys where literacy does not have a significant impact is Manual Arts, but an aptitude for Manual Arts won't take you very far these days.

Here is a conversation I had recently with a high school
P.E. teacher.

JM: *What percentage of P.E. is practical?*
Teacher: *Roughly fifty percent. The rest is general
theory, study of anatomy, tactics, stuff like that.*
JM: *Boys would need adequate literacy skills to get by
then?*
Teacher: *Definitely! A lot of guys get caught. They
think P.E. is all about getting out onto the ovals.*
JM: *So poor reading skills can hold them back, even in
P.E.?*
Teacher: *Some of them fail because of it.*
JM: *What sort of numbers are we talking — for those
who struggle because they can't read well enough?*
Teacher: *At this school [a private boys' school], two or
three in a class of thirty.*
JM: *What about other schools you have
worked in?*
Teacher: *At another school I worked in [a Catholic
boys' school catering for special needs] I would guess
about fifty percent. Before that I was at a large State
high school. There it was closer to seventy percent who
were struggling. They could have done a lot better if
their reading and assignment writing were up to scratch.*

Employment

As well as being a predictor of poor academic performance in high school, poor literacy levels and a reluctance
to read are also strong pointers to unemployment as an
adult. The age of the unskilled job has vanished for
Australian workers. Once, a boy could leave school at
fourteen, find a job by turning up at the factory gate,
and learn what he needed to know 'on the job'. Then,
the difference in wages between the skilled and the
unskilled worker was less marked than today. A man
might even progress into management purely on the
basis of experience and hard work. Reading did not
seem important during the working day.

This is no longer possible. Today, a 'skilled em-
ployee' is one with qualifications that almost certainly
require adequate literacy levels. Apprenticeships are
often offered only to those who have completed Year
12, and even then a good pass is needed to be in the
running for a position. There are sound reasons for this.
Most apprenticeships now involve significant theoret-
ical work as well as practical skills, and courses are
conducted in TAFE college classrooms. Some form of
study or training after Year 12 is the norm for almost
any field of work, and management positions require a
tertiary education. University entrance is highly competitive and a pass in high school English is essential.

But in the rapidly changing world of work, the
most telling consideration in regard to reading ability
and employment is this: throughout a working life of
forty years, the young worker starting out today is

likely to seek retraining for new jobs a number of times as the older categories of employment disappear. Indeed, this imperative has been building for decades already. Reading will undoubtedly play a vital role in this retraining, and those with poor literacy skills or a sense of reluctance towards text will be the least able to adjust.

Visual literacy

Much is made of the predominance of computers and the need for computer skills in employment. Boys excel in this area, and young men seem to dominate employment sectors wherever the use of a computer is integral to the job. Even though girls outperform boys in Year 12 results, more boys than girls end up in well-paid positions after leaving school, particularly in technology-related areas.

Some interpret this to mean that we are focusing on the wrong skills in our schools, and that the subjects schools devise are not as useful in the workforce as certain innately masculine skills and interests.

'Visual literacy' is often mentioned in this context. Visual literacy refers to the many ways that communication occurs through image rather than text; it is reading without words. The advent of popular magazines, television, video games and the Internet have made this form of literacy an important part of accessing and interpreting information. Consequently, it is important for education and employment, and schools have hurried to incorporate such skills into their curricula. Many boys are way ahead of them.

However, advocates of this 'new reading' can get carried away with their enthusiasm for visual literacy. As useful, and indeed essential, as this skill has become, it is an extension of and support for conventional literacy — not a replacement for it. For someone who reads regularly and who has built up a wide general knowledge through that reading, it is easy to ignore how much of the meaning or significance of an image is reliant on information already gleaned from the text.

Let us take the example of two boys who have been asked by their teacher to trace the history of the motor car. Together they quickly find a two-page spread in an information book with detailed pictures of cars, from the earliest horseless carriage to the latest Ferrari. Without needing to read a word, the boys can see the changes in aerodynamics, passenger comfort and safety, and engine technology. Or can they? The words and concepts just cited need explanation beyond what the pictures provide. One of these boys has read a magazine article about cars and had a discussion with his father about what 'aerodynamic' meant. He is able to interpret the changes in car body styles in these terms. The second boy thinks the older cars were just designed in an old-fashioned way. *Wind in the Willows* was read to the first boy years before and, recalling Mr Toad, he looks at a 1908 roadster and the attire of the passengers with a sense of recognition, noting detail, and understands why such clothing was necessary. The other boy, who lacks the additional information gathered from a wider employment of literacy, feels no connection to the picture.

The boy who has read widely can relate what he sees in pictures to information he has gathered from reading or interacting with text. Even though both boys are looking at the same pictures, the second boy is 'blind' to the full range of visual information available. This is confirmed when we look at the boys who go on to succeed in the technology-related careers where visual literacy is so vital. On the whole, the young men who occupy these well-paid positions have not emerged from the sea of boys who struggle with conventional literacy at high school. There is no evidence that poor literacy skills can be compensated for by computer or visual skills.

As an interesting postscript, let me add that one third of all students currently studying technology subjects at tertiary level are female. A gender balance may be only a decade away.

The well-read man: an influential citizen

These days, we are bombarded with information. Yet I am not the first to point out that information is not knowledge — and it is knowledge of important issues that is needed by both leaders and ordinary citizens in order for them to make wise decisions. This wisdom comes through acquiring information and the knowledge of others from a wide range of sources, and weighing the contradictions against one another through intelligent analysis.

Unfortunately, television news offers only brief

snippets of information through 'sound bites' and little more. Commercial current affairs television and talk-back radio programs provide 'infotainment' which serves up populist commentary in pursuit of ratings.

Whether to lead a community or to take up a citizen's right to share in decision making, people must look further. While some in-depth commentary is available through the ABC and SBS, the most effective medium is print, in the form of major daily newspapers, books and the Internet.

But ideas and information should not be accepted simply because they appear in print. Despite a rigorous editorial process, inaccurate and misleading information can still appear in books. Other forms of media are even more prone to bias and unsubstantiated state-ments. Many newspapers and magazines are biased towards certain political, economic and social ideals. With more and more information now delivered via the Internet, where anyone can make their opinions look like an expert's, the potential to be misled is compounded. (Some Year 7 students of mine set out to research the life of Martin Luther King using the Internet. The first two 'hits' produced by the search engine were wild conspiracy theories about his assassin-ation, and the third a tirade by a white supremacist.)

'Critical literacy' is the term used in education circles to describe the skills required to 'read between the lines'. It is this critical literacy that allows a person to detect bias and to make judgments about the author-ity or worth of a piece of text.

The leaders of a community, whether political, commercial or social, need access to a range of information if they are to develop a sophisticated understanding of the issues they must address. Since the most valuable and detailed information is to be found in print form, strong literacy skills are needed if effective critical literacy is to be brought to bear on texts. Without strong literacy skills, a man or woman may be locked out of leadership roles — or, if they do rise to leadership, they risk making poor decisions based on misinterpreted or misleading information.

Further, the ordinary citizen needs to stay abreast of current issues to guard against poor decision making by leaders. Therefore, strong literacy skills are essential to the upkeep of democracy and freedom — the literate citizen is a free citizen.

Reading and the imagination

Imagination is the ability to think beyond the immediate needs of our lives. As such, it offers release from the mundane and brings hope that tomorrow can be different and somehow better. Our ability to imagine has seen Homo sapiens grow from primitive foragers to become what Shakespeare called 'the paragon of beasts'.

Sometimes, though, I doubt our status as paragons blessed with powerful imaginations when I meet students who seem afraid to put pen to paper during writing workshops. While others are scribbling away happily, I try valiantly to coax a single idea from these reluctant participants. 'What if this happened …?' I ask, or 'Can you imagine that …?' They stare at me as though I had asked them to walk on the ceiling. Invariably, when I inquire, these students do not read.

Reading makes it easier to imagine because it opens you up to the new and unusual, and the remarkable concept that the impossible may be possible. Imagination needs input if it is to be set free. It needs to be stimulated and nourished by dozens of sources — film, television, computers, conversations, the observed experience of others … All of this adds up. But whether the imaginative focus is scientific or romantic, deeply personal or encompassing all human experience, reading offers the widest range of stimuli.

A rich and satisfying life

'Growing up ... involves the idea of the civilised man, the full man and woman with fitness not only for earning but more so for living and leisure.' So said prominent educator Sir James Darling in a 1993 address to the Australian College of Education, decrying education's 'present, rather banal purpose of making men and women more efficient instruments of productivity, competition and the increase of the gross national product.'

So far, I have explained why boys need books and reading in uncompromisingly practical terms. Adequate literacy skills enable a young person to reach his or her potential as a scholar, worker and citizen. In such achievement lies the basis of security and self-esteem, two of the most deeply rooted human needs. But there are other equally important and equally satisfying aspects to reaching one's potential in life which have nothing to do with school marks, employment or civic duties. As Helen Rose Gillan puts it, 'Children need life skills as well, especially in a culture of increasing leisure. They need to learn how to understand themselves and to develop worthwhile relationships with other human beings.'★

Dozens of commentators have expressed similar sentiments over the years. Work, power, wealth and material possessions are not a guarantee of happiness — yet in the drive to see that their sons have every

★*Storytime: Learning to read with Australian stories* Melbourne, Spectrum Publications, 1998: p.10

opportunity to succeed in life, it is easy for parents (and fathers in particular) to forget this. Perhaps it is an accident of timing. By the time most boys reach middle primary, their fathers are well into their thirties. The excitement of youth and those early years in a career have matured into the 'hard yards'. The pressures to achieve are great and the frustrations many, for it is at this stage in a career that promotion or success — however it is measured — is up for grabs. It can seem that to lose focus for an instant, to take any road not aimed directly at a practical, measurable goal, jeopardises one's position in a competitive world.

In turn, it is easy to transmit this view to a son who in all probability is destined for a similar road. The result of this blinkered view, passed on from father to son, is that reading is prized only as a functional skill which can lead to dominance in the manly world of work. To read for pleasure or enlightenment in the broader sense can seem an indulgence and, therefore, a waste of time. It is not 'doing something'. It is sitting around doing nothing, being lazy, spine-bashing. Yet it is in reading for pleasure, and to pursue personal interests with no apparent value or purpose, that the full man can emerge with a greater sense of himself and the world he lives in: human, spiritual, emotional, environmental.

Our boys have the right to be more than cogs in the wheel of a commercial society. Schooling which treats them in this way lets them down, and parents who look only for this narrow outcome when judging their son's skills and talents have let their boys down as well.

Literature (and other subjects like it) can have a human-ising influence, and has much to offer the development of masculine identity and personal growth.

Literature and reading for pleasure will not help your son get a job. Literature and browsing through a range of books will not make your son rich in the commercial sense. What literature *can* do, if supported and valued by you, is help your son gain a heightened awareness of himself in a complicated world, and give him a deeper understanding of what it is to be human. The deepest human experiences are expressed and explored most often through reading and writing. Knowledge, ideas, stimuli to the imagination — all contribute to a broader outlook and more satisfying life. Ultimately, this may make your son richer throughout his life as a boy and man than any school prize, sporting achievement or job promotion.

'People literacy': boys, girls and fiction

You have the right to feel a little suspicious of a subheading that stresses fiction. As well as being an experienced teacher librarian, the author of this book is also a novelist, after all. Is this where his true colours are revealed? Is the rest of this book devoted to the virtues of novels and ways of cajoling, tricking, begging, bribing or compelling boys into reading more of them? You are in for a surprise. Yes, narrative fiction certainly can play a valuable, though not exclusive, role in the enrichment of life — but it can also offer something more specific.

What do girls get from reading fiction that boys miss out on? If the answer is nothing more than an enjoyable leisure activity, which is what a lot of boys believe, then we need go no further. Boys have hundreds of enjoyable 'pass-times', most of them every bit as safe, satisfying and good for them as reading. But girls do more than pass time when they read. They learn about people.

Girls gain a great deal of their knowledge and understanding of human beings through the novels they read. They use fiction to become more 'people literate'. This does not necessarily come from the relationship novels so despised by boys. Any novel, whether it is a romance, a fantasy or a rollicking adventure, adds to the reader's store of experience in how people feel, think, behave, react under stress, display courage or struggle with personal dilemmas.

Such experience is the currency of human inter-action and understanding of self. On the whole, boys are not rich in this currency. Fiction offers a way into the bank vault. Today's boys are growing towards a manhood of which new skills are demanded. To fulfil the roles expected of partners and fathers, becoming 'people literate' is essential. And let us not forget that the same concept has become part of management practice when dealing with staff.

Fiction can also be a vicarious travelogue. There are novels set in almost every nation on earth and in almost every historical period. The randomly acquired detail of cultural practice, geography and real historical events and personalities becomes part of the reader's general knowledge. In turn, this helps a growing mind to make connections and understand the context of something encountered years later. For example, after our older daughter read *Playing Beatie Bow* by Ruth Park, my wife read it to our two younger children. Some years later, we holidayed in Sydney. Much to our delight, we found that a highlight for the children was our stroll around The Rocks, where the story is set. A feeling for the 'place' and a strong sense of Australian history from that period will remain with our children for the rest of their lives. Good novelists, Ruth Park foremost among them, pride themselves on the accuracy of detail in their stories.

So, do boys need to read like girls? Is that what this is about?

No!

Boys certainly need to make fiction part of their reading diet. But, arguably, girls could learn a little in return from those boys who do read. For all that many girls make good use of their reading to become 'people literate', there is growing disquiet that a devotion to fiction exclusively works against their best interests. It is a valid concern. Once, the education of girls was seen only as preparation for marriage and motherhood, roles in which 'people literacy' is very valuable. Technical literacy, experience of a wide range of reading material and a sound general knowledge were not considered important. Thankfully, such attitudes no longer constrict girls. However, an exclusive preference for novels may be continuing the disadvantage without girls realising it.

School students who read nothing but fiction may get through a prodigious number of books. They may even win English prizes. But they have narrowed their reading interests and experience to a harmful degree. Political, economic and social empowerment comes to those who use their skills to engage the full range of reading material available — from information books, biographies and newspapers to magazines and comics.

The aim, then, for both boys and girls, is a healthy balance. In this way, young people — whatever their sex — can become both 'people literate' and empowered in the wider world. Fiction has much to offer within this balance, but it is by no means the only form of literature to be valued.

CHAPTER TWO

Why don't boys read?

To offer solutions to any problem, we need to understand why that problem exists. This chapter attempts to get to the bottom of the reluctance to read so many boys exhibit. There is no single answer, no one change we can make which will sweep away our concerns. For some boys, their reluctance is intertwined with poor reading skills — yet there are others who have learned to read adequately but still decline to do so. What is holding them back?

As with so many longstanding and intractable problems, people have thrown up plenty of their own explanations over the years. I have heard them all and put forward a few myself. More recently, though, I have tried to cut through the conventional wisdom which has hindered a deeper understanding of many boys' reluctance to read and looked closely at the research. What I have discovered as a result of both my reading and my observations from many years' experience in dealing with reluctant readers is that the issue is a good deal more complicated than many people realise. The problem is rooted less in the fact that boys have so many other interests competing for their leisure time, and has more to do with society's expectations of boys and masculinity.

The usual suspects

Sport

It is not often that sport is painted as 'the villain'. Everyone sings its praises, from loving parents keen to raise active children to government ministers who seek the cost-saving benefits of a fit and healthy population. Who would argue with them? Sport is great. And when it comes to why boys do not seem to read very much, sport is usually the first reason trotted out. 'Boys are into a lot of sport and this takes up all their time and energy.' Such statements are often made with a wistful acceptance that this is just the way it is. But it is not.

Sport and reading are not mutually exclusive in a boy's life. We know this because many boys who play a lot of sport, even champions at the highest level, still read a great deal. It is also common to find that many reluctant readers are also sporting duffers who engage in little or no physical activity at all.

We need look no further than girls and their sporting habits for an enlightening comparison. Sport has always been a part of girls' lives, far more than is recognised by the media or society at large, yet no one is saying that girls do not read enough. Some girls now match their brothers in time spent training and playing, yet their enthusiasm for a good book remains.

No, when it comes to reading reluctance among boys, the time spent training for and playing organised sport is not the problem we think it is. If there is a problem with boys, sport and reading, it stems more from the myth that a sporting boy will not be interested in books and, conversely, that a boy who reads a lot must automatically be the non-sporting type. Somewhere along the line, this assumption has hardened into a solid expectation.

But why, when it is so clearly false?

Busy lives

Running alongside the assumptions we tend to make about sport and reading is the argument that children, particularly boys, are simply too busy to read. Again, sport is usually named as the culprit.

But in judging how busy our children are, we must be wary of counting only those hours spent on physically active pursuits. It is wrong to ignore things like keeping up with friends, a vital and time-consuming part of life for many children, especially girls. Girls are every bit as busy as boys. (Mothers of mixed families will tell you girls are the busier sex.) They manage to juggle school work, friendships, family responsibilities, their own sporting pursuits and, when they get older, work and romantic relationships as well. Yet despite their busy lives, girls make time for reading, while boys — in *their* busy lives — do not.

Having said this, the busyness of our children's lives should not be dismissed as an explanation for why so many children do not read much. Reading does take time. Rayma Turton, editor of the children's literature magazine *Magpies*, talks about 'time to be bored'. This is not the negative concept it might seem. I prefer the expression 'down time', meaning those periods — twenty minutes here, a few hours there — when there is nothing happening, no one to play with, no one to ring, no television. This is important time in the life of a child. It is a time to reflect, to be solitary, to recharge the batteries — and it is in this time that picking up a book becomes an option. It is in what little down time adults manage to find in the week that they can read for pleasure. Children are no different.

Sadly, many parents see it as their role to ensure that their offspring are never bored. As a result, their children never have down time. There is never a minute in the day when the child is not under the structured care of a teacher, coach or supervisory adult of some kind; there is always a task to perform and, therefore, something to do. Reading is not seen as doing something. It is not 'being busy'.

The child who likes reading will make the time to read. For the child who is ambivalent or has never given books much of a go, reading becomes lost in the rush.

Ron Jobe, a lively Canadian expert in children's literature, once asked an audience: 'Who has difficulty finding time to read?'

Much of the audience dutifully raised their hands.

'Aha!' shouted Dr Jobe. 'Of course you can't find time to read. No one ever finds time lying around as though it were lost. You have to make time.'

Television and videos

Television is an insidious competitor for reading time. Unlike organised sport — which usually takes place outside and away from the home — television is always there, available at the flick of a switch. Television never ends. There is always something to watch, no matter how unsuitable or banal, and it is easy to put it on, surf the channels and settle on something. Even when there's 'nothing on', there are always videos. It's a great way to 'veg out'.

Television occupies the same space and time as reading, and to a large extent shares the same purpose — to relax and entertain. Good television can even enlighten, inspire and challenge children in the way the best books do. Unfortunately, much of what is broadcast is shallow and instantly forgettable. The tragedy is that children rarely discriminate between good television and bad television.

Before electronic technology took hold, procrastination was said to be the thief of time. For many modern children, television is the thief which has crept unnoticed into their lives and stolen their spare time. In a lot of households, television has become not so much a childminder, since the parent is present elsewhere in the house, but certainly a child pacifier. That most tiresome of questions, 'What can I do?', is rarely heard when the television is on. One of the common answers to this nagging complaint used to be 'Read a book'.

Parents who would like to see their sons read a little more at home must ask themselves if their son is always able to choose to watch a television program instead of reading a book. If so, then perhaps television is robbing that boy of books and reading.

Preferred activity	Boys	Girls
Watch your favourite TV program	24%	35%
Play a new computer game	49%	20%
Read a really good book	17%	43%

1994 survey conducted in England across all school age groups

Video games

The table above shows that video games are even more popular than television among boys. Leaving aside arguments about the violent and gruesome nature of some games, many video games are a welcome addition to the growing list of entertainments available to children. Part of their appeal is their interactive nature, which means that they are not simply viewed in a passive way, like television. Many are complex problem-solving exercises, though if we are to 'get real' about this, we'd have to admit that most popular games are not. Unfortunately, video games have the same potential as television to steal large swathes of a child's spare time, reducing even further the likelihood of reading being seen as an alternative pastime.

Not enough books for boys

'There are not enough good books for boys' is a complaint often put forward to explain reluctance to read. Whether this common lament is true or not is a tricky thing to decide. Both publishers and the university academics who monitor such things insist it is not true, and they have a strong case.

Though girls do read more than boys, publishers have been deliberately targeting boys for some time. Increasingly, novels feature boys as the main characters more often than girls. Publishers are in a win–win situation here, because boys tend to avoid books about girls, while girls will happily read books about boys. It is true also that non-fiction titles tend to deal more with boys' interests than girls' interests.

So the real issue is not as easily identified as this. Watch an adult trying to help a boy find a book in a bookshop, particularly a novel, and you will discover it can take a while. Do the same in a school library and you had better pull up a chair. Yet it must be conceded that writers, publishers, critics and booksellers are making every effort to ensure that there are enough books for boys available.

Looking for new suspects

A round-up of the usual suspects — those competing for a boy's leisure time — is ultimately not very satisfying. They only go part of the way to explaining boys' reading reluctance. There must be more to it.

Gender difference:
what are little boys made of?

Beware of pop psychologists bearing maps of the brain!

The many differences between men and women make for endless and intriguing debate everywhere from dinner parties and office towers to school staffrooms. Assumptions about these differences have long been absorbed into the collective consciousness of whole societies, often to the detriment of one or both sexes. Feminism has taught us how much these assumptions have oppressed women. For example, it was once confidently proclaimed that women were too emotional to hold positions of power, and education was denied them because it was thought that their brains would 'overheat' if forced to think too much.

None of this was ever tested in a scientific manner; rather, it was considered to be 'commonsense'. Though our own age prides itself on sound scientific practice, individuals, or even entire communities, still fall prey to unproven assertions — the claims that seem to be commonsense. Worse still, our devotion to science can be used against us. Advertisements for shampoo or facial cream invariably claim to be 'university tested', and naive investors still sink money into miracle diet teas on the basis of 'scientific data'.

With advances in technology, much new data has been collected about the human brain. Part of this research has identified minor differences in structure and function between the brains of men and women, and the manner and speed with which they develop through the early years. That such neurological differences exist is not under dispute. However, a number of pop psychologists have hurried into print claiming that these differences explain various 'male' traits, including aggression and competitiveness, emotional withdrawal, lack of compassion — even marital infidelity and the failure to do housework. Could the difficulty that many boys experience in learning to read — and, indeed, the reluctance of so many to read at all — find its cause in such differences?

We need to be cautious here, for these psychologists have taken valid discoveries in one field (neurology) and used them to create a raft of new theories in another (behavioural science). These theories so far lack the rigorous testing that science demands. Notably, the very scientists who have identified these neurological differences are not making any assertions about what these differences mean. What should make us particularly wary is the way some commentators have pounced so gleefully upon this research as a means of supporting a wider agenda, often to shore up male behaviours that are perceived to be under threat from feminism.

It may well be that when suitable tests are developed

and further research carried out, we will discover that 'brain difference' does have a significant influence on the aversion to reading that so many boys exhibit. But let us be honest about this. The jury is still out, and until the link is proven, we need to explore other possible causes.

Testosterone

The same pop psychologists who peddle untested theories about brain difference often throw up the male hormone testosterone as the irresistible force behind the behaviour of men and boys, especially teenage boys.

As both a respected psychiatrist and a faculty member of the Harvard Medical School, Dr William Pollack can presumably be trusted to know what he is talking about. This is what he has to say about testosterone:

'The level of testosterone in any boy — and the way that testosterone affects him — has less impact on his behaviour than how that boy is loved, nurtured, and shaped by his parents and by the context of the society within which he lives. The hormone may well predict a certain type of energy in boys. But the way in which that energy is funnelled and expressed lies in our hands.'★

★*Real Boys: Rescuing our sons from the myths of boyhood* New York, Henry Bolt, 1999: p.56

Real men don't read

Just as science has continued to explore the body and brain of humankind, so has it delved into the way we form and regulate our societies. This has led to debate about why males and females behave differently. The evidence points strongly towards a surprising conclusion: that behavioural traits long assumed to be naturally 'male' or 'female' are not laid down in our genes at conception, but are actually taught to children by the society they live in. In jargonistic terms, this process is called 'gender construction'. I have never been a fan of jargon, though, so I will do my best to avoid this label in what follows. However, the ideas put forward under the umbrella of these two words provides the most convincing argument yet to explain why many boys would rather have their fingernails pulled out than read a book.

Here, in simple terms, is how the argument works. How does a baby boy become a man? Physically, his body is programmed at conception to grow automatically towards manhood, passing through certain recognisable stages along the way in a process controlled by hormones unique to his sex. He need only wait around for twenty years or so and his body will have done the business for him.

But how does a baby boy come to *behave* like a man? The same does not follow. There is nothing automatic about this part of masculinity. The hormones which trigger bone and muscle growth and the development of sexual characteristics do not teach a boy how to behave. A boy must learn how to act as a man, and he does it in the same way he learns to speak. He watches and he listens to the people around him. He creates himself as a man by copying the models of masculine behaviour presented to him.

At the heart of this proposition lies the belief that society starts to teach boys how to be men from the very moment they are born. It is not an activity carried on in classrooms; it happens informally — even unconsciously — every minute of the day as the trial and error of interaction with their world teaches boys what is expected of them. The models of manhood boys are exposed to are essential to this process — and this is where the first problems with reading reluctance occur.

The behaviour most often presented to boys is the stereotyped form of masculinity endlessly perpetuated in the media and on the sporting field. This is a model revering physical activity, strength and ascendancy, a model in which the successful male is powerful, solitary and dominant. There is no room for reading in this model. In fact, in its narrowest form, this model of masculinity dismisses books and reading with contemptuous disdain, and puts pressure on those who aspire to be successful men to do the same.

Reading as a feminine activity

Why is reading dismissed so contemptuously? Let us observe the young boy in his early years. He quickly learns that there is a difference between 'acting male' and 'acting female'. The word 'acting' here is chosen deliberately, because selecting certain behaviours according to gender does involve performance. Young boys learn that to be identified as a boy by others, they must perform as one; they must walk the walk and talk the talk.

The most obvious model of masculine behaviour in these early years is a boy's own father, but there are plenty of others — grandfathers, uncles, older brothers, the characters in the many television programs he watches, and even the stories his parents read to him. As he grows older, the culture of video games, adult films and adult television will become powerful influences. Ultimately, though, the most intimate and influential factor for many boys, as both the model for their behaviour and the judge of their performance, will be their peer group.

As early as their first playgroup or kindergarten, many boys discover that one effective way to build and maintain a masculine identity among their peers is to reject anything that appears feminine. This is reinforced every time they exhibit unmanly behaviour and are told not to be a sissy — or worse, are hit with that ferocious and much feared insult: 'You're a girl!' For such boys, the seeds of reading reluctance are planted early.

A few simple questions reveal why.

- Who is most likely to read bedtime stories to a boy?
- Who teaches a boy how to read?

- Who sits with a boy through the laborious 'read–aloud' stages when he is learning to read?
- Who is a boy most likely to see reading a book?
- Who is most likely to encourage him to read?

The answer to all of the above is 'a woman'. So at a time when many boys are busy establishing their masculine credentials by proving that they are not feminine, who do they find to be very much concerned with books, reading and story? The women and girls around them: their mothers, sisters and female classmates, their teachers and the librarians who support them. Books are a female preoccupation.

Reading is a learned behaviour, just as cooperating with the teacher and trying one's best in class are learned behaviours. If they are perceived as inherently feminine behaviours, boys keen to underpin their masculine identity by rejecting the feminine will develop and maintain a poor attitude to books, reading and possibly schooling altogether.

Good literacy skills — reluctant readers

I have been careful not to claim that all boys develop such a clear and uncompromising view of reading as a feminine behaviour which threatens their masculine identity. Many, perhaps even a majority, do not. More to the point, many of those who do score well in reading tests, and enjoy the approval of mothers and teachers for doing so, are still reluctant to read when given a free choice. Let us turn our attention to these boys and see where books and reading lie in their construction of themselves as masculine.

Whether or not a boy adopts a contemptuous disregard for the feminine, it still holds that the most common models of masculinity presented to him are the stereotypes of the sporting field and the mass media. A young boy's heroes are most likely to be the triumphant sportsman (Wayne Carey, Michael Jordan, Shane Warne), the Hollywood soldier (Sylvester Stallone, Jean-Claude Van Damme) and the rebellious celluloid policeman who pursues vengeful justice through unorthodox means (Clint Eastwood, Mel Gibson). These are the names of the last decade or so. The names were different decades ago and will continue to turn over with the years, but the exploits and images of those held up as the pinnacles of masculinity will probably not.

It is common to hear young boys claim the identity of the current stars when they play in the backyard. A boy picks up the bat and he is no longer himself. He is his cricketing hero, transported in his mind to the middle of the MCG, where he blasts a faultless century for team and country. (At eleven, I invented an entire touring party from a fictitious nation which came to do battle with Bill Lawry's Australians.)

The dominant masculine models performed for boys to emulate revolve around a culture of activity and physical achievement. Most boys find their masculinity judged by what they can do, either in organised sports or through informal competition, involving pursuits like skateboarding, bike riding or fighting. A boy's masculinity is rarely judged by what he knows or what he can achieve sitting on his backside — the exception, perhaps, being prowess in computer games.

Being judged by others and receiving the positive reinforcement that stems from 'having a go' is an important way for boys to build self-esteem. Hence, the self-esteem of many boys is inextricably linked to being active, to getting out there and doing things.

This is why athletically inclined boys often have an oddly hot and cold relationship with books about sport and sporting heroes. They are certainly attracted to such books, and the teacher or librarian who walks into a classroom with a boxful will have no trouble 'selling' them. But the appeal is not the information or story that the book contains — rather, it is the promise of the dream. Diagrams and tips from the experts will not hold a boy's attention for long. The story of a great sportsman's life and career will do better, but can still lose the interest of even the most avid sporting boy. It is the action photos which draw the eye, stirring excitement and demanding to be shared with others. For boys raised in a culture of activity, such books are an aid to worship. Then the book is closed and they all go outside to see how well they can play the game, just like their heroes.

Where does this leave books and reading? It leaves them outside the culture of a boy's life. For a boy looking to build his self-image through what he can do with his body, books offer nothing. For a boy seeking the approval of others for his physical achievements — especially the praise and acceptance of his father and his peer group — reading offers nothing. For the boy who aspires to dominance over his peers through leadership in their activities, books and reading are irrelevant.

If boys are reluctant to read, it is because they have been taught by the society they live in that books are not an important part of their lives or their identity as males. Arguments that books and reading are essential to their futures, couched either in terms of career opportunities or enlightenment for the soul, mean nothing to them. Such concepts, no matter how much they concern teachers and parents, simply do not rate alongside the more immediate adventures in a boy's life. We should not judge them harshly for this. But nor should we sit quietly by and let this reluctance to value books and reading go unchallenged. The stakes for boys and the society they help to influence as men are too high.

Challenging the stereotypes

Boys are not reluctant to read as a result of any innate physical or psychological factors peculiar to their sex. The major part of their reluctance is learned, both as a resistance to what many perceive to be a feminine behaviour, and as disinterest towards an activity deemed irrelevant in the lives of men and boys.

To reduce such reluctance, we must make some adjustments to the way we socialise our boys. Firstly, we must break down the perception that books are for girls and women. In conjunction with this, we must challenge the stereotypes which dominate our boys'

lives and lead them to believe there is only one kind of man to be respected and admired. Put in such simple terms, it does not seem like a difficult task. But let's not fool ourselves. Many men find such stereotypes comfortable, and others, such as advertisers and sports promoters, find them useful for their own ends. At least some of these would view any efforts to institute change as a threat to either their position in the social order or their personal performance of masculinity.

The biggest challenge, then, is to show boys that reading does not threaten masculinity but enhances it. You might have your own list of masculine qualities that you admire. For what it is worth, here is my list (in no particular order): strength of character, a sense of personal and collective responsibility, a compassionate outlook, tolerance of difference, a profound respect for women, a devotion to achievement. (My list of feminine qualities does not look much different.) A boy can use reading to develop and enhance these qualities. By reading stories about heroes who face adversity with courage, determination and integrity, a boy's own fledgling character is given a wide range of models he might aspire to. Good writing, by delving into the humanity of characters, promotes an understanding of others as well as the self, supporting the values of tolerance, acceptance and compassion. The action or performance we call 'achievement' is underpinned by taking on skills and information, and preparing oneself. Reading can be a vital part of this process. It can give a boy the edge in creating himself as a man to be proud of.

Books and reading are hardly going to inhibit any of the qualities included on my list. Nor for that matter are they truly capable of inhibiting sporting prowess, a strong competitive instinct, courageous leadership, loyalty to mates, or any other positive masculine qualities you care to name. Yet the perception and the suspicion of many boys is that reading does weaken their masculinity. If we want a culture of reading to exist around our boys, we must lay these myths to rest.

Educating boys

It is now well established that learning to read starts very early in life; some would say even before a baby has arrived home from hospital. With the first words a child hears, he begins his progress towards language, towards understanding what others are saying and making words of his own so that others will understand him.

There is also ample evidence to show that from the time they are babies boys and girls are not treated in the same way in this progress towards language. Girls are spoken to more often than boys. Boys are tossed around in physical games more than girls. Girls are encouraged to vocalise and practise communicating through words, while boys are encouraged to act and challenged to *do* things more often than girls. Along with that encouragement comes expectation. Boys quickly learn what is expected of them, and they understand how important these behaviours are for love and approval. Though the expectations held by parents, grandparents and others are often unconscious, the overall effect is still the same. Before they embark on the formal road to reading, boys are not as well prepared as girls to cope with language.

There are any number of simple research projects which point to the way male and female children are treated differently from an early age. I recall reading an interesting example in a newspaper article some years ago. Infant boys and girls who were crawling but not yet able to walk were allowed to move around on a tabletop while their parents watched to make sure they didn't fall off.

Whether the watching parent was a father or a mother, the boys were consistently allowed to venture closer to the edge than girls before intervention occurred. The implicit assumption was that boys had a greater need to make judgments about danger, and so the parents — mothers as well as fathers — allowed them to experiment and take risks.

Whether we like it or not, our perception of the future behaviour of our children and how best to prepare them for what will be expected of them is riddled with assumptions based on gender.

The culture of schools

Differences in attitude and expectation of boys and girls are woven deeply into the informal fabric of our society. What about the more formal institutions we have established to socialise our children, in particular our schools? Some commentators have argued that curricula and teaching practices have become feminised. By this, they mean that schools now reflect the interests and practices of females to the disadvantage of males. Some go further, muttering darkly that this is part of a deliberate process of bringing about gender equity in the wider community. They point to the high proportion of women in the teaching profession, and changes in teaching practice that have seen lessons move away from fact and certainty in favour of a greater emphasis on research skills, individual discovery and an open-ended approach to knowledge and learning. Those who have led these changes defend them on the grounds that such an approach is better suited to the modern world. The detractors claim it disadvantages boys.

In my view, there is no deliberate gender bias operating within our schools aimed at advancing girls ahead of boys, and I certainly support the curriculum reform which has taken place. At the same time, I think it is reasonable to ask if there are factors in the culture of today's schools and the way students are taught to read which do not match the traditional culture of boys.

One person who has written extensively about the reluctance of boys to read is English researcher Elaine Millard. She has identified a range of factors which seem to create a reading community in schools that is more relevant to girls than boys. Australian schools and teaching practices are very similar, and these factors are certainly present in Australian schools as well.

There is a heavy emphasis on fictional story, Millard has found, in the material used to teach reading — both in the early instructional phase, and later, when regular practice is the focus. Even books which are designed to give information still present that inform-ation in the form of a story. While boys do not dislike stories, the significant men in their lives are most often seen reading newspapers, magazines and work-related material. They expect reading to have an informative or practical purpose.

As well, the types of literature which teachers see

as inappropriate are actively discouraged. The computer, sport and hobby magazines which boys bring to school are usually not permitted as reading material in class, and as for comics and other material which boys do read for pleasure, the teacher can be downright disparaging to the point of banning them altogether.

At the same time, when boys are given free choice in their reading, the material available to them in the classroom is narrowly focused on what teachers approve of, and little advice or further intervention is offered by teachers. I consider the point Millard makes here so important, I will quote her verbatim:

> *Once children could 'decode print' and had worked their way through a reading scheme, they were frequently left to develop further reading strategies independently. The general assumption was that children would grow individually towards reading more complex texts. There was little monitoring of their subsequent progress except for asking them to complete the lists of titles and page numbers recorded in diaries along with a smiley face or star-rating system. Poor readers often remained on reading scheme books which reinforced their sense of failure and which repeated the same pattern of syntax and narrative structure.* *

* Elaine Millard, 'Differently Literate: Gender identity and the construction of the developing reader' *Gender and Education* vol 9, no 1: p.32

From Year 4 onwards, reading practice is given low priority during the school day, often being confined to the fifteen minutes after lunch when the children are tired from racing around. In many schools, this time is formalised into a program with a title such as USSR (Uninterrupted Sustained Silent Reading). Such time is vital and should be a feature of every school day. Unfortunately, even this time is easily undervalued as some children are assigned to clean out a cupboard or collect sporting equipment, while others are expected to catch up on written work. The implicit assumption is that written work is of greater importance than reading. All this contributes to the view that time spent reading like this is actually unimportant, even to the teacher who says otherwise.

It is hardly any wonder, then, that boys become confused. On the one hand, they readily accept that reading is important for 'getting started in life', but on the other, the school reading they engage in is mainly stories intended as a leisure activity. 'Where is the purpose?' they ask. For when it comes to leisure, they have many alternatives they enjoy far more. Some boys, at least, see themselves as being forced to take part in a female leisure activity — one that a boy would not choose freely.

In late primary and early secondary school, the set book for class study begins to appear. This is not necessarily a bad thing in itself. (My own interest in reading was sparked by the novels set in Years 11 and 12 at my school. Before this, I had read little.) But the choices available are often narrowly centred on literary novels or other genres which boys do not favour.

Some teachers would dispute the assertion that their choice of novels is narrow, claiming that they have bent over backwards to accommodate boys. However, the telling questions are: Couldn't a range of options be available rather than a single text? and Why is the class book always a novel?

Practise, practise, practise

It is wrong to conclude, however, that reading is completely forgotten after the initial years of instruction. In fact, children are implored to read, read, read in order to practise and strengthen their skills.

It is only right that this be so. In fact, it is essential. Reading is a skill much like kicking a football. If you want to get good at it and stay good at it, you have to practise — get out there with a footy and kick it. For reading, to get good and stay good, you have to sit down and read. There is no other way.

Yet, as Elaine Millard discovered, the school day is busy and the syllabus crowded. Some reading time after lunch is as much as a primary teacher allows. In secondary school, it is rarely possible to spare any time at all. Through necessity, reading practice becomes a homework activity.

This means that at a time when a boy most needs to improve his reading skills through practice, the responsibility for that practice is thrown back onto him and his parents. This is where the progress of many boys falters. Through no conscious fault on the part of busy parents, reading practice is all too easily allowed to slip. It is often seen as an add-on if time remains after the serious business of written homework has been completed. But for a boy who desperately needs this practice, it should come first. It is not easy to get a boy to do it, either, particularly if he is struggling, has an indifferent attitude and is not slow to use all the usual avoidance strategies.

It is not just struggling readers who fall back here. The same problem can occur for boys who have responded well through the first three years at school. The failure to follow through with practice in the middle and upper years of primary school will leave them languishing with a slow reading speed and a piecemeal exposure to half-finished books. The table displayed on page 18 shows that the percentage of boys reaching an acceptable reading standard actually declines between Years 3 and 5. This needs special emphasis, because poor reading skills are a major factor in the reluctance that so many boys show towards books and reading. A vicious cycle is created. Reluctance to read sees a boy avoid the practice he needs, so his reading skills fail to develop, thus making the act of reading more laborious. This heightens his sense of failure, prompting an even greater reluctance.

The multiple whammy

This chapter has put forward a range of reasons to explain why so many boys are reluctant to read. No one of them is the sole cause of a boy's reluctance. Instead, they combine to create a 'multiple whammy' effect. It is not the same set of factors for every boy, and some may avoid them all. But parents need to be aware of the attitudes and practices which influence their sons and turn them away from books and reading.

By way of a summary, here is a worst case scenario for how it might happen to one boy. In his first three years, the boy finds his parents delighted by everything he does physically, but they do not encourage or extend his talking. Mum reads to him, but she rarely discusses the story before, during or after the reading. He does not connect the black markings on the page with the story he hears, and he has little awareness of words around him, on signs, cereal boxes or his Dad's shirt.

At preschool he plays with everyone at first, until on Grandparent's Day his grandad expresses surprise that a boy would enjoy playing with girls. From then on, he plays only with boys. They do a lot together. There is not a lot of talk and they never talk about themselves, only about what they are making or doing.

At school the next year, the teacher talks about words and sounds, but he does not understand much of this. How can that funny black shape make a sound? The girls seem to know, but he is not a girl. He does not like it when the lady, his teacher, tells him to pay attention. He is a boy like his friends, and they would rather be outside playing. That's what boys like. Not girls' stuff like letters and the sounds they make. He gets into trouble for not doing the right thing and his friends laugh. He likes them to laugh. He laughs when they get into trouble too.

He starts to dislike reading lessons. It is a struggle, trying to remember what sound a letter makes or what a word looks like. What does he have to learn all this for anyway? His dad doesn't have to read anything. His dad knows everything. He wants to be like Dad.

Now that he is in Year 2, his mum is always getting him to read at home. It wouldn't be so bad maybe, but he can see how frustrated she gets when he doesn't know the words. If he holds out long enough, she will give up and let him go out to play. If he can get away without reading he does, and because Mum and Dad are busy, this happens a lot.

Ah, the end of Year 3. He won't have to read anything for six whole weeks. Great. He knows he is no good at it anyway. In fact, he hates reading books. TV and Nintendo are heaps better.

Next year he starts going to the remedial teacher, but he just doesn't like reading, and can't see the point really, so he doesn't try. Besides, he is into footy and the swimming club now. He is too tired even to do the reading homework his teacher insists on.

His friend gives him a comic some time in Year 5. The words aren't hard and the pictures help — it is pretty cool — but his teacher confiscates it because he is reading it during art. His teacher is a man now, and he thinks the cricket magazine is a good thing to read during Silent Reading. But that was cancelled yesterday because they hadn't finished their maths problems, and now his mate has borrowed the magazine. In the next reading period, his teacher gives him a baby's book to read instead because it matches his reading level. He won't even look at it.

He is in Year 6 now, but his reading has not improved for years and he cannot keep up with social studies and maths because of this. He reads nothing at home, and at school he reads only when someone stands over him. Last week, his teacher wrote on his report card: '... is struggling in all areas. A reluctant reader.'

For many boys, a reluctance to read is inextricably linked to poor reading skills. Such poor reading skills are often the cumulative effect of a lack of oral language development in the early years, the poor attitudes towards reading resulting from social constructs of masculine behaviour, schooling practices and resources which seem less suited to boys than girls (or certain boys, at least), and the neglect of reading practice both in the classroom and at home through the vital first five years of school.

The factors above which relate directly to the school are largely beyond the scope of parents to influence. Even for teachers change is difficult; they are presented with a curriculum and expected to get through it. Flexibility is limited and one might reasonably point out also that the system manages to work quite well for most girls and a good number of boys.

However, parents are capable of doing a great deal to address the difficulties boys encounter and the reading reluctance such difficulties create. The next section of the book offers detailed advice on just what parents can do to build a culture of reading around their sons.

PART TWO

The stages of development

CHAPTER THREE

From birth to starting school

If you have a son only a few months old and you want him to read well and willingly throughout his life, then I have caught you just in time. All the research shows that a boy begins to acquire literacy skills from the day he is born. He will not meet a preschool teacher for three years, and it will be five years before he turns up for that first day at school. But by then, his fate as a reader will largely be sealed. This is an incredibly bold statement — but I stand by it, and most teachers experienced in the early childhood years would agree.

It follows from this that the role of parents is paramount. The attitude of parents towards books and literacy, and their actions in the pre-school years, is the most important factor in determining how well a child will learn to read and write when he does reach school. It will also have an overwhelming influence on his attitude towards books in those early years of primary school, providing the platform — though, unfortunately, no guarantee — for continuing positive attitudes as he moves out of his parents' orbit and falls under the influence of his peer group.

So what should I do for my son? asks the anxious parent.

A world of words

A child begins learning to read when he begins hearing the human voice and learning to talk. These should not be viewed as separate and distinct endeavours, but as part of the same process, gradually building on what has gone before. Encouraging a child to make sounds, holding 'conversations' even when the baby cannot actually utter a recognisable word, is important. This is by no means unusual behaviour among doting parents, certainly, but some fathers may choose not to participate (missing out on the pleasure it can bring) in order to maintain masculine dignity. But it is a serious business. The encouragement to make sounds, any sounds, and then the positive reinforcement of smiling and more warm sounds from the parents, brings forward the learning of language.

Observation of parents with infant children has shown that boys and girls are treated differently. Boys are manhandled more, lifted up, tossed about, while it is girls who are more frequently encouraged to vocalise. So give both sexes a fair go. Give your daughter more time *in* the air and your son more time *on* the air.

Restricted versus elaborate language

Interacting with young children through language has enormous benefits for their schooling. This interaction must encompass more than the functional dialogue heard around the house as children express their simple needs, and in turn receive brief instructions about what they should and should not do. Where this is the only language children have been exposed to, they arrive at school with a limited vocabulary and a poor understanding of how words fit together to make meaning clear. They also tend to rely on gestures, facial expressions and half words to make their meaning known. Their experience of language is restricted, and the number of words they can use and recognise by sound may be only a third that of a boy who has been exposed to a richer dialogue.

> Talking with your son can happen at any time:
> - When you are sharing a book, all sorts of informal discussion can go with it. ('Why is the frog so sad?')
> - When you are out and about together, you should encourage your son to notice and name things. When he shows an interest, talk about them. The earliest words he recognises will be the ones which help him to make sense of his world.
> - When grandparents and friends come round, there is the chance for him to

experience one-on-one conversations with
people from outside the house.

A boy's experience of language will grow steadily
through hearing and experimenting. Only through
trying things out can he develop more complex sentence patterns and discover a wider range of words to
describe things. In this way, he becomes better at
expressing his thoughts and personal needs through
words rather than gestures or actions. This means he has
developed an elaborate form of language.

All schools operate in a climate of elaborate
language. Boys with restricted language experience are
disadvantaged before they walk in the gate. Consider
two boys who come across the word 'bantam' in their
reading. Neither has seen the word before, but one
knows what a bantam is because he once overheard his
parents talking about the chickens Grandma keeps
penned in her backyard. The other boy does not know
what a bantam is, and when he is told what b-a-n-t-a-m
creates as a word, he still does not know that it means a
type of chicken. While the first boy makes the connection and so moves on untroubled in his reading, the
second stands still. If this happens continually, he will be
a long way behind.

The focus of reading readiness in preschools is to
widen the experience of language so that this does not
happen. But even the best preschools cannot do the job
as well as the home environment.

*Research has shown that the
day-to-day vocabulary heard in
the average home and on
television uses between seven
thousand and ten thousand words.
The high school student is
thought to need a vocabulary of around one hundred
thousand words if he or she is to succeed
academically. Winston Churchill used half a million
different words in his seven-volume history of the
Second World War — and still managed to leave
many in the dictionary untouched.*

A world of print

You may have noticed in preschools and infant
classrooms the many charts and posters on the walls, or
the cards with single words on them used to label
things like doors, windows, bookcases and so on. This is
not because there is nowhere else to store the chart —
nor because the teachers keep forgetting the names
of things. The intention is to create a world filled with
the printed word. Children then become comfortable
having words around them. They notice the shape of
them and, through natural curiosity, may well ask what
particular words are. Such children are ready to read.

You do not need to make your home look like a
classroom, but the same principle applies. Colourful
posters with words on them, alphabet friezes around the
walls, notices stuck to the fridge, useful phone numbers

pinned to a corkboard — all of these things play their part. So do alphabet toys, jigsaw puzzles with words in the picture, games with written instructions, fridge magnets in the shapes of letters, or a sign on a boy's bedroom door with his name on it. Then comes the actual reading material: the books on bookcases (and, if your family is like mine, lying around on chairs and under coffee tables), magazines, department store catalogues, junk mail, comics, newspapers, school newsletters — anything that has words printed on it.

Children will notice these words and comment on them when you are at the supermarket or driving in the car. ('What does that say, Daddy?') It may take a second to identify what has caught his eye. Then you tell him, explain a little of what it is there for, and praise him for noticing it. From this he learns that words have not only a meaning, but a purpose. He also learns that his parents think it is a good thing that he know about words, and he earns your approval for wanting to know.

Reading to your son

It will come as no surprise that reading stories to children is vital. The plea that you read to your son will be repeated many times throughout this book. Reading stories is a powerful way to build his experience of language and share the joy of books and reading. Books open up a much wider vocabulary and variety of sentence structures than the daily speech of the household. Even when a child is too young to understand the story, the sound of your voice, the play that goes on with the book, the intimacy and the recognition of Mum and Dad's interest in the book are what count.

A world of books

Over time, children should have access to a wide variety of books and stories. It is a great idea to join a library. Lifelong membership of a library supports lifelong reading. Public libraries will let you borrow a dozen picture books at a time.

Having a large number of books in the home has been identified as a reliable pointer towards good and willing readers, so owning books and building up a collection is very important. It should begin from the earliest years by buying books yourself — either new or second hand — and by encouraging friends and family members to give books as presents. A book box should be part of a boy's bedroom furniture from the time he moves from the cradle to a cot. Later, when he moves into a real bed, he will need a bookcase to store his books. Ownership of books means ownership of reading. Personal books are there all the time and become favourites. A boy's books will end up like his teddy bear — dog-eared, dirty, with bits torn and missing. Like a teddy, this is proof that the book is loved.

The question of quality

The quality of a picture book is important. Though texts are short, creating picture storybooks is actually a sophisticated art, taking into account the rhythm of the words, the interaction of words and pictures, and the style of illustration. Virtually all picture books stocked by libraries will meet these high standards. Unfortunately, some television spin-offs and the cut-price books sold in supermarkets can lack this attention to detail.

Do not be deterred, though. Ultimately, the quality of a book is just the icing on the cake. The important thing is that you have books, any books, to share with your child, ready for the precious time you spend sharing the experience of reading. If supermarket books are the only ones you can afford, go for it. There are some excellent titles available at discount prices.

Consider this, too. A book you made yourself, with your son watching and helping, will have amateurish illustrations, poor layout, cheap paper and not the greatest story-line in the world — but the time and interest you invested in it is of enormous significance to him. So on a wet afternoon, when you are looking for an activity to occupy a bored son, create a picture story-book together.

Parent/child interaction around a book

Variety and quality become important when you consider the interaction which takes place between the child and the book, and the discussion that can revolve around it. Sharing a book with a young child is about more than reading the words on the page while he looks at the pictures. It is about creating meaning, relating this to the child's experience, and watching him grow as a literate person through the process. Is it any wonder that this interaction may need intervention and help? Discussion of the book before, during and after the reading plays an important role in the acquisition of language skills.

Language is used:
- to predict what will happen through guesses, looking at the pictures, thinking about the title and any hints it gives, and speculating about what will happen in the end when you have reached the middle of the book;
- to analyse what has happened, why, and in what order;
- to clarify, when things become confused, by asking questions or going back to an earlier page;
- to make connections between parts of the story, linking cause and effect;
- to draw conclusions when the story is over.

This requires time, patience and subtlety. It is not about comprehension, but experience and interaction. It is not about stock questions or procedures determined by the adult, but being sensitive to the signals coming from the child that something extra is needed. Of course, such interaction should never get in the way of fun. Kids should enjoy it, and you should enjoy reading to your children. You will not have the opportunity for such intimacy with them for long. (Note — the books in List 1 on page 192 have been chosen for their appeal to both children and their parents.)

Bedtime — anytime

In some families, one parent — often the father — does not arrive home from work until a boy is in bed. Shift workers may have the same difficulty. But why does shared reading have to be a bedtime activity? It can happen any time — ten minutes here, twenty there, on weekends and holidays. Such times also afford the opportunity for those important one-on-one conversations that increase a boy's experience of elaborate language. Children should know that reading is not confined to bedtime. They will soon learn that the enjoyment of being read to and the intimacy that goes with it can be had at any time. Expect your son to roll up beside you, book in hand. 'Read to me, Daddy,' or 'Tell me this story, Mummy'. When it happens, count yourself the lucky parent of a son likely to enjoy books and reading.

Story structure and repeated readings

Reading stories to children gives them a grounding in story structure — the beginning, middle and end — which all stories conform to, and which the child will eventually be asked to reproduce in his own stories. If he has shared, on average, four stories a week every week for the three years before he arrives at school, then he has heard around six hundred stories! More than ample as a start, I would think.

Cut that figure back a bit, though, because there is great value and great enjoyment to be had in repeating stories. ('Read the crocodile one again, Daddy. It's my favourite!') From favourite and oft-repeated stories comes more detailed appreciation of language and wider discussion. Memory and prediction come into play, along with the pleasure of hearing a favourite part once again, either for the action described or the very words used. (*The Enormous Crocodile* by Roald Dahl ends with the words: '... where he was sizzled up like a sausage'. My son loved to say it with me, the 'sss' sounds emphasised with much delight.)

Let your son have a say in the choice of book. When he develops a favourite, demanded a dozen times in as many days, try leaving out a few words or changing the story in a small way. He will pick you up on it, perhaps even tell you off indignantly. More discussion, more use of language, more awareness of story structure and the purpose of words.

Not all reading is stories

There is a tendency to think that all books for young children must be in the form of a story. As explained in chapter one (see pages 32–3), this narrow view can cause problems. A great many of the world's books contain information rather than stories and children need to know this. *The Baby's Catalogue* by Janet and Allan Ahlberg is for very young children, yet there is no story, simply pictures linked by theme. It is important for both boys and girls that they are introduced to information books and the vicarious fun and interest they can bring, whether the topic is dinosaurs, animals, fire engines or the human body.

Other reading activities

Reading books is not the only reading activity. These are some other activities which might flow naturally from the reading of a book. They can be used to demonstrate the relevance of reading in the wider world.

- Draw a picture together from the story.
- Make up a story from a picture that interests your boy.
- Make up a story with your son as the main character.
- Read from the children's section of the paper, inviting comment and making connections to your son's own experiences. A child's first interest in newspapers is often the cartoons. They recognise that the pictures represent some kind of story. They see words associated with the pictures and want to know what they say, realising that the words must tell the story too.
- Invite your boy to share your magazine or a coffee-table book. The interest may last only a few minutes, and will centre on the pictures, but identifying the mass of print and associating it with the print

he has seen in picture books is important.
This also shows that not all print is
narrative.

Modelling attitudes

Here is a sobering thought for the parents of boys. In
the last chapter, it was noted that boys and girls are
unconsciously treated in different ways by their own
parents and those around them. Studies have indicated
that boys are expected by their parents to be less
knowledgeable about print and less interested in it than
girls. The implication is clear. You must expect your son
to share your interest in print. If you do, he more than
likely will.

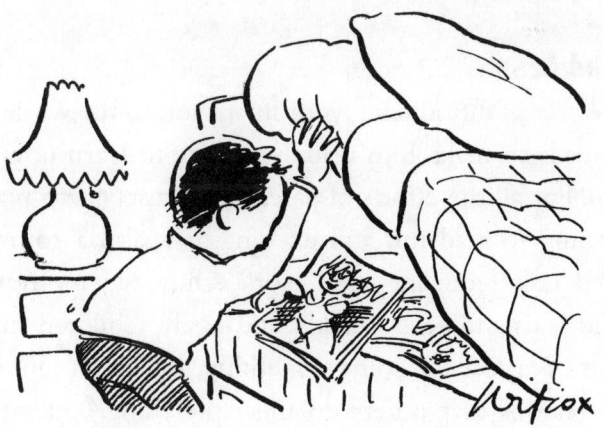

Some years later, Max
discovered that his father
was, after all, an avid reader.

Reading to your children demonstrates, in the strongest possible way, your own attitude towards books and reading. By making time for it in a busy round of chores, you show your boy that it matters to you, and so it will matter to him. It shows that books are a subject of interest. Your child will learn and copy your interest. Coupled with the sight of you reading occasionally, this demonstrates the everyday nature of reading and presents it as an activity that he can take on for himself. He will be busting to get to school so he can finally learn this skill. He may even demand early lessons from you. More than a few boys have taught themselves to read before their Year 1 teacher ever sets eyes on them, though it is important that the boy himself initiates the learning. If you have made him ready to read, then under the guidance of his Year 1 teacher he will be reading soon enough, and your role, though still significant, will change.

Preparing for school

Readiness

The aim of introducing your infant son to the world of words is to make him ready — ready to learn how to read. For all the efforts of parents and teachers to make learning to read fun and exciting, it is also a complicated task requiring hard work. Only the motivated child learns to read quickly and easily. Children must have a purpose for doing something, and understanding the reasons that others do the same thing builds this purpose. Reading readiness is about centring that purpose within the child's own world through activities that mean a lot to him. The more he sees it as a personal challenge, the more he will take it up as a challenge. In a few words: 'reading is an attitude more than a set of skills'.★

Attitudes to school — attitudes to women

Only a fool would undermine the authority and importance of a teacher in the eyes of a young boy. Perhaps it is unnecessary to make such a blunt statement. The consequences seem obvious — a boy will not learn much from a person he does not respect. Whether a father or a mother, you might well bristle at the suggestion that you would do such a thing. But while such undermining is rare in an obvious sense, how much of it occurs indirectly? Most Year 1, 2 and 3 teachers are women. If a boy has already been strongly encouraged to show his masculine identity by 'acting the man' — by adopting his father's view that women and feminine things are something he must separate himself from — then not only has his teacher (a woman) been put at a disadvantage, the boy himself has been disadvantaged in the classroom.

An important part of reading readiness is making a boy ready for school and ready for his teacher. He should know what to expect and he should be excited about it. This happens by talking positively about school

★Paul Kropp with Wendy Cooling, *The Reading Solution* London, Penguin, 1995: p.56

and teachers in the years leading up to his first day, taking him to see his school, and meeting his teacher beforehand, if this is possible. Much of the rejection of books and reading that boys exhibit is linked to a rejection of school. Starting with and maintaining good attitudes towards schools and teachers is crucial for positive attitudes towards reading.

Schooling has changed, and many of the humiliating and niggling practices which current parents may remember from years ago have ceased. So take a look at your son's school before he starts. Most schools will gladly agree to interviews with parents intending to enrol children, even twelve months in advance. This interview will include a tour of the school. Take your son along and let him see that school is a bright and happy place.

We all want our children to do well at school. We all want our children to read. Perhaps it is not too optimistic to hope that everyone reading this book wants children to respect and learn from their teachers, whether male or female. What we need to realise is that these three desires are intertwined, and we will not achieve one without the other two. To do the right thing by our boys, we need to accept our responsibilities towards all three goals.

CHAPTER FOUR

Learning to read — Years 1 to 3

The last chapter made it clear that learning to read and establishing a positive attitude towards books and reading begins long before a child starts school. However, the actual process of reading is taught in the first three years at school. These are the all-important years when the readiness is turned into an essential life skill. Classroom activity will never focus more completely on basic literacy skills than it does throughout Years 1, 2 and 3. If your boy does not learn to read well now, he faces a serious struggle to acquire the literacy skills needed for the rest of his formal education, for wide-ranging employment opportunities, and for all that an interest in books and reading has to offer.

The parent/teacher partnership

You have been involved in making your son ready for reading. Now it is time to see that involvement bear fruit. What is needed is *more* involvement.

In the teaching of reading, the teacher teaches,

then comes the practice. With, on average, twenty-five children in an infants class, much of learning to read is a whole-class activity: reading Big Books, and learning and repeating the sounds and symbols that lead directly to the decoding of words. This comes easily to some — but not so easily to others. A great deal of repetition and practice can be needed to master each step.

The teacher tests or monitors her class carefully to gauge the progress of each child, re-teaching where necessary, until she judges it is appropriate to move on. While she does her best for each child individually, uppermost in her mind are both the curriculum to be covered in a limited time, and the best interests of the class as a whole.

A teacher is rarely able to get round to each individual child to conduct the one-on-one practice that some children need. Teachers' aides and volunteer parents help in and around the classroom but even then the ratio of children to adults is still high. The best chance for one-on-one practice is in the home. Parents are partners with the teacher in the teaching of their own children. They do not need extensive training or experience; it is not the role of parents to do phonic drills at home. If the teacher does ask you to do such extra work, she will probably supply materials in the form of a fun game.

What parents need to give is their time, their patience and loads of encouragement to see that the practice is done and that their child does not fall behind. Parents of boys must be particularly aware of this for, whatever the reason, boys seem more prone than girls to falling behind. But don't panic. It is more than likely that your son simply needs more time to master each step in what is, after all, a highly complex skill. I have avoided the word 'failure' here deliberately. Taking longer to learn such a skill is certainly not a sign of failure. Boys will come through as long as they have patient and dedicated parents willing to maintain their half of the under-recognised partnership between home and school.

How to help at home

Build on the interest in print and language already established

Let your son know that learning to read matters to you, his parents — and especially his father — and so it will matter to him. Show him that you think this is a skill a man needs, a skill to be proud of.

So talk about it. 'How was school today? Show me what you did.' Even in the first weeks of school, writing on a child's drawing what he says about it is a common technique used by teachers. When he brings that drawing home, you can double the effectiveness of this by asking, 'Did you draw that picture? It's great. Tell me about it. What are these words written underneath it? What do they say?' He can't read them, but he will tell you what they say, and without correcting him, you will nod and thank him. You might even add a few words of

your own, telling him what you have written or asking him if he has anything to add. This is reading practice.

There are dozens of such exercises. Teachers have their favourites, and they may well outline them to you at a parent/teacher night early in the year. Fathers should not leave attendance at these meetings to mothers — your son will notice the absence and presume his father is not interested in what a female teacher has to say. You do not have to understand the detail or become a teacher yourself. Your interest and enthusiasm will convey itself to your boy and keep him committed to this earnest business of becoming a man who reads.

Ask about the story that the teacher read to the class that day

Another common practice throughout the first three years of school is the daily class story. Good teachers vary these with information books as well. Reinforce the influence of this practice by occasionally asking about it. That day's story may have struck a chord with your boy, leading to extended discussion. Alternatively, he may not even recall what it was about, in which case you needn't pursue it. It doesn't matter. Fathers take note — through your interest, your son will understand that it is okay to share his enthusiasm for something he heard from a book with this strong masculine presence in his life. It is as though you are holding up a sign: 'Books are cool for men and boys.' Later, with similar encouragement from you, he will want to share what he has read himself. Be prepared to have your ear bent.

Such interactions should never be thought of as comprehension or memory exercises. They are shared discussions, man-to-man or boy-to-mother. You will marvel at your son's capacity to absorb detail. For this reason, it is a good idea to practise looking interested. Believe me, at times the re-telling of stories and the recount of detail about dinosaurs and space craft can be excruciating! But this is reading practice. No doubt about it.

Be sure to give story a chance too. Showing a bias towards his interest in information, rather than story, is to plant the seeds for your boy's rejection of fiction when he is older — and this rejection can seriously retard the speed and effectiveness of his reading.

Have your boy read aloud to you (and understand the error of errors)

This is a task for both parents, both to share the load and to reinforce perceptions that reading is masculine or, better still, gender neutral. If Dad is unable to do his bit because he is not around at 'homework time', then another time can be found. It is better if such reading does not look like homework, anyway.

The way you listen and respond to errors made by your son is critical. Do not correct every error he makes, as he makes it. Research has shown that this common practice is not necessary, and can quickly lead to frustration and a sense of failure. Simple errors such as 'of' instead of 'for' should be ignored altogether unless the error occurs every time. In such cases, a jovial comment at the end of a page is all that is needed. ('Do you realise you have been mixing up these two words?') Such errors sort themselves out as more reading is done and children begin to read with a greater awareness of context and the overall meaning of a sentence.

Of course, more serious errors can change the meaning or render a sentence meaningless. Bring the child back to this at the end of a sentence or paragraph — wherever you feel it is most appropriate. Ask him to try it again. He will have a better idea of context by then. If he still makes the error, or simply doesn't know the word, don't make him try over and over. Tell him the word immediately; if it is a new or unusual word, talk about it. Talking about it will help him remember next time.

When a boy hesitates, stumbles or makes an error with almost every word, then the text is too difficult and he should not be made to continue — again, avoid frustration and failure. If this too-hard text comes from a book supplied by the teacher, the teacher needs to know. A simpler book will be substituted the next night or, if the reading skill is not yet there for even the simplest sentences, flash cards and work on basic sounds and letter combinations may be more effective.

Be aware that reading aloud is hard work
Think about those early years of reading. The child soon starts to recognise simple words, but he still has to shape his mouth and tongue to speak them. At the same time, he is trying to create meaning by continually checking context. Added to this, in each sentence he meets a few words that he is not sure of, either because he has never seen them before or because he has not yet learned to recognise them on sight. He has to attack such words with his new reading skills, decoding the letters to make sounds and matching the combination of sounds with a word he knows. Then he has to check the context again and finally utter the word.

Sounds tiring, doesn't it? Is it any wonder, then, that as you watch kids struggle through just a few lines, you will see them yawn, pause to catch their breath, swallow built-up saliva or comment mid-sentence about the illustrations? The yawning is not a sign of boredom but of tiredness. The pauses and the deep breaths are a sign of the effort being expended. Respect your son for the effort he is putting in and let him know about it.

As hard as it is, you both have to stick with this practice until the child has worked up an extensive vocabulary of words he can recognise on sight. Only when he reaches this stage can a sense of reading fluency be achieved. It is when the decoding of the text becomes an unconscious activity, occurring in 'the background', that the meaning and significance of what is being read can move to the 'foreground' of consciousness.

Short bursts are better than extended practice

Because reading can be so tiring and frustrating to the young learner, regular short periods of reading practice — say about ten minutes each time — are better than half an hour all at once. This is consistent with the way most skills are learned and improved anyway. You must be the judge of how long each session should last for your son. There is little benefit to be gained once a boy starts to squirm and lose concentration.

A common way to extend sessions and maintain the sense of fun and achievement is to share the reading. He reads the first paragraph on a page, you read the rest. It is a trap to believe that every word in every book supplied by the teacher or selected from the library must be read by your boy.

Not all reading practice has to be oral

As noted above, the process of reading aloud is complex and tiring. If the need to speak the sentences aloud is withdrawn, the reading becomes easier and the child can focus more fully on the meaning of the words.

Part of reading practice is letting your boy read a few paragraphs silently. He might need to ask you about a few of the words or the meaning of a difficult phrase, but given the opportunity and a little help from you, he can manage on his own. It is important to stay with him, though, as a companion in the reading, perhaps reading a paragraph here and there to speed things along. A few carefully placed comments or questions from you will soon show how he has fared. Full comprehension is not necessary. If he has 'ownership' of the reading, he will want you with him, to show what he has achieved and to help him through any confusion.

From here, he can move on to more independent reading, but the sharing and the monitoring should continue — the first so that reading continues to be a pleasure for him, and the second so that you can be satisfied he is completing the task and comfortably handling the sense of what he is reading.

Be a reader yourself

This is a contentious issue. It would seem merely commonsense that the children of parents who read will become readers themselves. However, the research indicates that there are no guarantees. There are still many avid readers who lament their son's disinterest and, conversely, many cases of non-reading parents whose sons read extensively. Add to this variations within the same family where, with the same model on display, one son reads everything and the other nothing. What is going on?

The simple answer — as discussed in previous chapters — is that the influences on your son's attitude to books and reading are many, not just the model displayed at home. Nonetheless, you should feel reassured that reading parents *are* more likely than non-reading parents to produce sons who read. Alas, though I have seen no figures to support this, my feeling is that the model provided by fathers comes to the fore most powerfully when the boy is himself a man. So take heart from this and consider the long-term view.

In the meantime, remember that if you only ever read in bed after your son is asleep, then he never sees you reading and may be unaware that you do. So let him know occasionally. Show him your book, or mention that you are enjoying a particular book while you are interacting with him over his own reading.

What the research does show, however, is that whether a boy sees his father as a reader or not, his father's attitude is paramount. One sure-fire way for a father to destroy his son's interest in books is to say openly, 'I'm not a reader. Books don't appeal to me.' By implication, this tells a boy that his dad doesn't really want him to be a reader either. (After all, how many seven year olds support Carlton if their father barracks for Collingwood?) Attitude is all.

Avoid a sense of reading failure

The quickest way for a boy to dismiss himself as a reading failure is if his mum and dad think of him as one. Learning a new skill, whether physical or intellectual, doesn't happen overnight. Seen as a line on a graph, progress resembles a staircase, with brief periods of rapid improvement followed by 'plateau' periods of consolidation. The path to reading fluency is no different. There will be periods when it appears little progress is being made. If parents lose patience in these periods they can do great harm. Even the non-verbal signals of your frustration are easily picked up. Your son will become frustrated with himself and start to fear he is no good at this reading business. Yet his halting advance towards fluency might be no different from most of his classmates. Progress cannot be hurried because time is part of the process. Experience shows that regular practice over time is the only way to work through the plateau stage and make the next leap in fluency. Through these stages, your son needs your enthusiasm; he needs to hear small improvements applauded, to be supported when he seems discouraged, and to be praised for the effort he is making. Be pleased with yourself too. When finally you come through together, your patience and effort will have given him a gift as great as any he will ever receive.

Communication with the teacher

Education authorities around the world now recognise the importance of early intervention for children who do not develop adequate reading skills and the fluency that builds on them. If you think your boy is progressing too slowly or has stalled altogether, speak to his teacher straight away. Different resources may be made available to you that better suit his needs and interests. His problem may be quickly identified and, with a bit of re-teaching focused on his weaknesses and extra practice at home, he will be able to take that next step. This may be all that is holding him back. Ground lost in the first three years is very difficult to make up. Sadly, the evidence points in the opposite direction. The disadvantage grows steadily, year after year.

Keep on ...
Continue activities begun in the early years.

1. Keep reading to your son
Your son may learn to read quickly and be reading happily on his own while still in Year 2. It is a mistake to think this means you need not read to him any more.

Some of this reading may be integrated with the reading practice outlined above. But often this is not appropriate. Your boy still wants and needs the pleasure of being read to with no strings attached. It is a time he shares with you, and it is well worth the effort you make to maintain this special time.

The type of book will change. Longer picture

books can take two nights to read. Or perhaps this is the time to introduce chapter books — stories divided into chapters of ten or twelve pages, often with an illustration every few pages. (List 3 on page 195 has some suggestions.) Information books have a role here as well.

Books on tape

The range of books available on audio tape has blossomed in recent years. Public libraries are the easiest and cheapest place to get hold of them. They are a great way to extend the exposure to elaborate language that is so important and, because they are read by professional actors, they can be highly entertaining as well. For school-aged children, especially in middle primary, listening to a story on tape alone in a bedroom can be fun — a great alternative to video games or television — and it can take some of the pressure off busy parents. However, in all of this, do not lose sight of the importance of sharing books, demonstrating parental interest and building positive attitudes. Books on tape are a way of supporting such goals, not a substitute for reading with your boy; for this reason, they are not suitable for the very young. (Of course, for parents from non-English speaking backgrounds and for visually impaired parents, books on tape offer something they might not otherwise be able to provide for their children, and so my gentle warning does not apply.)

Books on tape can be great for long car journeys, such as the tedious drive to Grandma's at Christmas, and they certainly reduce that most nagging of questions, 'Are we there yet? Are we there yet?' Children will often hunt out the book to read by themselves on their next visit to the library. (My advice — get three or four titles for a journey, as some are more appealing than others.)

2. Keep building up a library of personal books

A boy's own books will usually reflect his development. However, there is great value in the information book or novel, well beyond his reading level, that grandparents or others give him. Though reading such books is beyond him, they represent his future and he knows this. He recognises the confidence the book-giver has in him. Browsing over the detailed illustrations found in today's non-fiction books can fascinate a boy even though he cannot manage the captions or text. He will ask (even pester you!) to be told what various words are. This is great stuff, made all the more valuable because he owns the book.

3. Keep going to the library

In chapter seven, I will go into more detail about the difference between books a boy can read for himself and books you will read to him. For now, it is enough to point out that boys will often pick books that are too hard for them. Some subtlety is required here. You need to explain *gently* that a book is too hard for him and he should choose something else. But this will not always work. Sometimes he is determined to have the book because it holds some significant appeal for him that he cannot explain. Let him take it. When he cannot read it, read it to him. If it is still well above his level of comprehension, and ultimately does not hold the interest he thought it would, you will judge the right moment to stop. His enthusiasm has not been diminished, and he has learned an important lesson. To read a book for himself, he will have to improve, and not all the best-looking books around are actually what they appear.

CHAPTER FIVE

Consolidation —
Years 4 to 6

This period in your son's development is where so many boys are lost to books. By the end of Year 3, schools expect children to have mastered the basic skills of reading. The assumption is that children will gradually build on those basic skills over the rest of their primary schooling to a point of fluency approaching adult levels. This means expanding a reading vocabulary from only a few thousand words towards the levels needed in high school, estimated at one hundred thousand words. It is not an unrealistic expectation and many do just that. Unfortunately, a worrying percentage of children do not, and a high proportion of these are boys. The failure to achieve fluency in reading can be a major factor in reluctance to read and poor attitudes towards certain types of books.

The middle and upper primary boy

Let us look briefly at the culture of boys in this age group, from Year 4 through to Year 6 — though, as ever, the boundaries are blurred. A boy is now much more independent of his mother. He spends large periods of time out of her presence, much of it at school or taking part in recreational activities with a circle of friends who play an increasingly important role in his life. His interests will largely be the interests of that peer group, certainly while he is with them. Despite your best efforts at home, your son's peer group may not value reading and, in extreme cases, might well be openly antagonistic.

This is a time when boys are renowned for their boundless energy. To give positive direction to that energy (and to maintain sanity), schools and parents tend to channel it into busyness, with a particular emphasis on organised sport. This encourages a strong identification with a father or other significant males who find sport to be a comfortable way of moving more fully into a boy's life. If the boy's mother has been his only link to reading, that link can be strained or broken.

What about at school? Depending on whole-school policy or the practice of individual teachers, there may be no time set aside for independent reading during the school day. Homework is moving away from oral reading in favour of silent reading. The reading component of homework will most likely be the requirement to read so many pages of a book each night. Amid the excitement of a boy's life and the pressures of the curriculum to pursue other important goals, reading can become lost — both as a skill to be practised in order to improve fluency, and as a source of entertainment and information.

Reading for fun and purpose

Before a boy starts school there is only one kind of reading — the shared reading where the parent reads and the boy listens, watches and comments.

Once schools starts, there are two — this same shared reading, and reading practice as the child reads himself, usually aloud. Sometimes there is a bit of cross-over, but not much. This creates a sense of difference between reading purely for pleasure and reading to improve a skill.

After Year 3 it becomes even more cloudy. Reading by parents to children for pleasure continues, or at least it should. Then there is the reading a boy is expected to do for himself — this is supposed to be both practice to improve *and* a pleasure. Where a boy finds no pleasure in such reading, it is difficult for him to maintain a positive attitude. At nine or ten years of age, it is hard to see any purpose in a demanding and uninteresting activity, especially when everyone thinks you should be enjoying it as well. If they are to keep reading, boys need to find fun or purpose in the act of reading.

- Reading a madcap story is fun.
- Browsing over (and intermittently reading) a well-illustrated book about aliens or dinosaurs has purpose.

- Reading a dog-eared book chosen at random by the teacher may well hold neither fun nor purpose. Only the motivated will stick with it.

Parents are essential at this stage. They are the ones who can keep a boy motivated so that the practice gets done. And they are the ones who must see that a third strand of reading is introduced and encouraged, if a boy does not introduce it himself. This is the personal reading that happens apart from parents and apart from school. If we are to build a culture of reading around our boys, parents need to nurture this personal reading so that a boy keeps reading willingly and widely through the middle and upper primary years.

A boy needs:
- *to maintain a positive attitude towards books and reading*
- *parents who remain intimately involved in his progress as a reader*
- *time to read*
- *a place to read*
- *access to a wide range of books and other reading material*
- *a home environment that controls distractions such as television and video games*

What parents can do

Attitude and involvement

Parents, particularly fathers — though mothers are vital here too — need to be involved in their son's reading by showing approval of his efforts, asking about what he has read, demonstrating an interest in it, and being open to discussion. Wherever possible, they need to be visible and enthusiastic in their own reading as well.

The most straightforward way of achieving this is by continuing to read to your son. He is past the simple story by this stage, and well into chapter books which might take more than a week to complete. Since you are reading to him, you are his key to novels and information books, and a level of language still too hard for him to read for himself but which he can under-stand perfectly. Lists 7 (fiction) and 12 (non-fiction) on pages 205 and 218 recommend some good titles. Staff in bookshops and public libraries will happily supply more if asked. The teacher librarian at your son's school can and should play an integral role at this stage.

As a more independent human being, a boy of this age will gradually discover his right to have personal interests very different from his parents. He will also discover, with your help, that these interests can be expanded by books. This is important because it helps to build a purpose into reading — and reading without purpose is like beer without bubbles. Its effect on attitude is fundamental.

Entertainment is not the only purpose of reading,

even for a novel. Boys and girls both use books as a gateway to the rest of the world, as sources of inform-ation and general knowledge. Be aware of this when choosing books for your son, either as suggestions for him to read himself or as books to read to him. Though he will want to be involved in the choice, you are still influential in the access he gains and the choice he does make.

Look for balance in what your son is reading — though take the long-term view. Boys are subject to fads as much as anyone and to read only one kind of book for week after week is not unusual. But when he seems to be stuck in a 'comfort zone' for months on end, the time has come to intervene. He may not be reading at all, and borrowing a book, any book, from the library is an attempt to cover this deficiency. At such times you, the parent, might need to bring home a range of different things from the library and encourage him to browse through them. If it is fiction that he baulks at, and this is common, try the 'sure-fire winners' from List 10 on page 213, perhaps reading a few pages to him before letting him take over for himself.

Teacher librarians

Most schools, both primary and secondary, have teacher librarians. The role they play in schools is often only vaguely understood by many parents and, for that matter, a few teachers as well. The general assumption among parents is that this person has a class like all the other teachers, but takes on the added task of staffing the library at lunchtime and buying, covering and shelving books.

In fact, teacher librarians are specialists, just like P.E. teachers. But where the P.E. teacher uses the ovals, the pool or the gymnasium as a classroom, the T/L uses the library. They are all experienced classroom teachers who later specialised in this field by studying for further university qualifications. Very broadly, their role in the school is:

- to manage the library collection and purchase new resources;
- to plan and teach information skills, such as how to locate information and make the best use of it;
- to help students apply these skills to tasks assigned by teachers; and
- to promote an interest in reading and provide a wide range of reading material to students.

The last of these roles offers valuable support to students whose interest in reading is waning through the middle and upper years of primary, and into secondary as well. The T/L has the specialised knowledge of reading material which classroom teachers may lack and can offer the guidance that teachers often do not. Parents concerned that their son is turning away from reading should consider speaking to the T/L and asking that a special effort be made to recommend books and other reading material to challenge reading reluctance before it takes hold.

Book Week

Children's Book Week in Australia is held in August each year. In this week, awards are made to the best books as judged by experienced librarians, teachers or other specialists. Along with these awards, books and reading in general are celebrated. Supporting the activities during Children's Book Week shows your positive attitude and helps engender one in your son. A common activity is the 'book parade', for which children dress up as their favourite character from a book. It can be a trial for parents, but valuable fun for boys in particular. Hamming it up is part of the entertainment.

This is often the week when writers and illustrators are invited into the school to talk about their work. Parents can double the benefit of such visits if they ask their son about what was said or done, and then see that he gains access to books by that author or illustrator through the library or by buying them for the home collection. This applies whether the visit is during Book Week or not.

I have a bone to pick with some school book parades. In recent years, many costumes have had more connection to television, movies and video games than books. This is particularly so among boys, and reflects their attraction to electronic entertainment. While not wishing to spoil the fun, I encourage parents and boys

to remember that this is a special week set aside for books and reading. It is both a chance to tell others of a book you liked, and a way to identify the good books that others have enjoyed. Hopefully, children will go on to read the favourite books of their classmates. This can't happen if Batman and Bart Simpson outfits dominate. Enough said.

Reading at home

In the home, you can provide vital support for any reading expectations that the teacher places on your son. You might need to approach the teacher directly to find out precisely what these are. If there are none, then establish your own. This is the time in a boy's life when charts, challenges and rewards work best. (More of boy-friendly incentives in chapters seven and eight.)

The busyness that we encourage in our sons can easily encroach on the time devoted to reading as homework — and surely missing one night can't do any harm. But to miss three or four times a week, week after week, will seriously disrupt fluency.

A place to read

At this age, place plays an important part in boys' lives. This is when they build cubbyhouses and discover quiet hideaways on creek banks or in what little virgin bushland there might be in the area. Place becomes personal. At this time, we are trying to make reading personal as well. So, with the full participation of your

A place to read...

son, set up a reading place — a place where he is comfortable, relaxed, has the level of privacy that suits him (some need quiet, others like a bit of companionship and noise while they interact with books) and, if possible, a spot to stash his books. Make this the place he goes to read. It might be in his own bed with a special pillow, a beanbag or something similar in the corner of his room, a particular chair in the lounge room or on the veranda, a nook behind the sofa, or in the master bedroom when Mum and Dad are not there.

A place for his books

Large picture books and information books are awkward on a standard bookcase. Many simply have to lie flat, if they have not already fallen over. They are more easily stored in a plastic book box in the early years. However, by now your boy is into chapter books and novels as well. He needs a bookcase in his bedroom. You may even build it with him. (My son helped me build his — a one-day job consequently took two!) Carpentry duffers will need to buy one ready-made.

On this bookcase go the books that were given to him by well-meaning relatives three Christmases ago but were much too hard for him then. He will discover them now in a quiet moment when he browses through his bookcase. This month's books from the public library can also be put there. There must be books in the house, books for his age group, plentiful and visible. This is where he will find books without making a special effort or a special trip away from the house, a trip which is becoming difficult to fit into a more independent and much busier life.

A time to read

In conjunction with a place to read, boys need a time to read. In chapter two I quoted Ron Jobe, who reminded his audience that to find time to read, we must *make* time. Parents must help a boy make time to read. The most obvious time is between when he gets into bed and when he turns out the light. It can be any time that suits your son, but it needs to be regular, encouraged and — as best as can be managed — immune from frequent disruption. In an earlier chapter, television and video games were named as competitors for the time a boy may spend reading. To free up more time — hopefully for reading — limits need to be set on how much television is watched. No TV during the week is a common household rule; if this seems too draconian, perhaps a bit of negotiation around the dinner table is in order. Children can pick out the programs they really do want to watch, but then the screen goes blank and reading becomes an option.

The same rules can be negotiated for video games, which are now of greater interest to boys than television. There is plenty of evidence that reading and electronic entertainment can coexist as part of a boy's life, but only where television, videos and video games are controlled.

The computer

Whether text is found in a book or on a computer screen, it is still text. While surfing the Net can mean aimless flicking from image to image, more controlled browsing to a series of known and interesting sites can entail a surprising amount of reading. Newspapers often list such sites in a weekly column, or the school or public library might circulate a list. Increasingly, schools have links to such sites through their own home pages — and you are not confined to the home page of your own school either.

Reading like this is linked to the excitement that technology always holds for children, especially boys. The fact that it seems entirely practical as well as fun means it has the added advantage of not appearing to

be reading homework at all. But it is reading practice.
And there is no evidence so far that using computers or
the Internet in this way alienates children from books.
Of course, balance is important — you should make
sure this isn't the only reading your son is doing.
(See page 171 for more discussion on reading and the
Internet.)

Access to reading material

Access to a wide range of reading material may well be
the most important of all points raised in this chapter.
The range needs to be wide because to read for pleasure
a boy needs to find material that he enjoys. Yet boys of
this age, like everyone else, are subject to moods and
fads and sudden changes of interest, the influence of
friends and a host of random factors that affect what
they want to read. Often a boy will simply not know
what he wants until he stumbles across it.

> Good schools support this need by:
> - scheduling regular sessions with the
>   teacher librarian so that books and other
>   reading matter can be recommended;
> - building into the timetable regular visits to
>   the library for borrowing;
> - stocking reading resources outside the
>   requirements of the curriculum;
> - supporting Book Week, book clubs and
>   book fairs.

But schools and school libraries have their limitations when it comes to boys and their preferred reading for pleasure, as we shall see. Parents and the home environment can be a far more potent force at this stage if they take up the challenge.

A boy's own stuff

The importance of building a collection of books within the house has been continually stressed. Hopefully, it will become a habit and an accepted — though not necessarily onerous — call on the family budget. As I've emphasised before, ownership of books means ownership of reading.

The subheading above was deliberately chosen to evoke memories of the *Boys' Own*, once a magazine of ripping yarns for boys. These days, you find the variation 'Boyzone' as an expression celebrating the boyish interests of our sons. A boy's collection of novels, non-fiction books, magazines and comics should be his own. It should contain favourites he has read more than once, and items he has swapped with others and may swap again. They should be a proud part of who he is, just as his cricket bat and football are his own.

He will be choosing his own book purchases by this time as well as still receiving gifts. As far as possible, purchases should not be confined to special occasions, and you would certainly want to avoid the idea that birthday and Christmas presents are always books. Is a subscription to a much-prized magazine out of the question? Since interests can change quickly, perhaps a better policy is to be open to occasional requests for a magazine, book or comic that connects with a new sporting interest or hobby.

Bookshops are not the only place to find reading matter for a boy to own. Newsagents, second-hand bookshops, book fairs, book clubs and swapping with friends all play their part in building up a personal collection that in itself builds a culture of reading around a boy.

The public library

If your son is not already a member of a public library in his own right, this is the time to get him his own card. A regular fortnightly or monthly time for visits will help. Public libraries have certain advantages over school libraries which more than compensate for the disadvantage of not being 'on the spot'.

- School libraries often have quite small borrowing limits of only two or three books at a time, on the basis that children can turn their books over every few days. Public libraries let a borrower take a dozen or more books at each visit. Encourage your son to bring home a bucket load. There is a comforting freedom in sitting in the midst of a nest of books, flipping from one to another — all of them your own choice — until you identify the one that suits you at that moment.

- Public libraries are open all year round, not just in term time. The summer holidays through December and January are a time when boys have more spare time than they know what to do with. Organised sport is often in recess over summer as well. Reading as a leisure activity is a strong possibility now, and parents beleaguered by bored children should consider a trip to the public library.

- Books held in public libraries are more likely to be in good condition. Budgetary restraints force school libraries to keep books on the shelves long after the pages have yellowed, the corners furred and the spines broken. Aesthetically, books in public libraries can have more appeal.

- In the eyes of parents, public libraries may not sound like fun places, evoking instead memories of drab, silent rooms and suspicious librarians. But increasingly they are now oriented towards technology, providing access to the Internet and CD ROMS away from home and school.

- Libraries are also becoming easier to access. The trend now is to locate public libraries in major shopping centres and extend their hours to better reflect the needs of busy readers.

- There is another regrettable factor to consider. Not all boys feel drawn to their school's library, which can gain a reputation as the refuge of the 'uncool'. Many boys visit their school library only with their class in lesson time, and borrow books only when directed to do so by their teacher.

CHAPTER SIX

The teenage years

If boys in the middle primary years tend to *fall* off the reading merry-go-round, many teenage boys *jump*. Teachers and parents see it all too often. Youngsters who have read eagerly across a range of material through primary school drift away from the habit of reading in secondary. (To be fair to hard-working secondary teachers and librarians, I should note that I have seen it happen the other way; non-reading primary students blossoming into enthusiastic readers in secondary school — but in general, the first phenomenon is more common.) This chapter is intended to help you arrest that drift, in part at least, and also to lessen any sense of disappointment if, in the final years of school, your son does drift away. The journey is not over yet and the ultimate prize might not be lost to you at all.

When it comes to reading in high school, you will find three kinds of boys — let's call them *functionally illiterate*, *literate* and *a-literate*.

Functionally illiterate

These are the boys who cannot read well enough to survive in high school — let's not beat around the bush. These boys are functionally illiterate. Their future is grim. They can be identified by these characteristics:

- a reading age many years below their real age (for example, a fourteen year old with a reading age of nine)
- a general rejection of books, and active avoidance of reading
- poor marks in school
- low self-esteem and lack of motivation in any school work that involves reading.

If you have just picked up this book, opened it at this chapter, and recognise your boy by this description, he desperately needs your help. He needs the intervention of you and his teachers. He needs a specially devised program of work at school and at home. The first step will be to check fully if he has any physical disabilities, such as eye problems, or cognitive disabilities, such as attention deficit or difficulties in processing symbols. This should have been done years before, but there are those who slip through the net. Take him to a specialist outside the school if you have to.

If his problem stems more from attitude than disability, then you will have to work on this, building his self-esteem and helping him to see that books and reading are both fun and relevant to his life as a teenage boy who will soon be a man. The males in a boy's life — his father, older brothers and even his friends — have a role to play in turning around negative attitudes. Chapter nine gives details of what can be done. In households lacking male role models, a concerned mother might enlist the help of male teachers or sporting coaches admired by her son, as suggested in chapter ten. Indeed, I view such positive and supportive attitudes as a fundamental responsibility for any teacher, whether he teaches English, maths or manual arts. Other strategies for parents are discussed in the chapters of part three, 'Reaching out to boys'.

Literate

Literate boys are ones who can read well and do so regularly of their own volition. If these boys apply themselves in high school, they stand every chance of doing well academically and finding both delight and enlightenment through their reading along the way. Oh happy day!

The parents' role here is to keep their sons supplied with books, to maintain positive attitudes, and to offer interest and encouragement. By this age, a teenager has opinions of his own and his reading will inform these opinions. You have a young adult on your hands. Every time you engage with him over something he has read — even when this engagement is better termed an argument! — you reinforce his need for reading. The first time a boy quotes an author 'or something he read' to support his argument, crack open the champagne. You certainly have a boy who lives within a culture of reading.

A-literate

There are many boys who can read to an acceptable standard, but drift away from regular reading to the point where they read virtually nothing that is not required by the school. I call them 'a-literate'. While they can get by, they do not progress as readers — not in speed, vocabulary or the vital area of critical literacy. This in turn compromises their academic performance and narrows their view of the world. These are also the boys who have difficulty studying and responding to narrative fiction as part of their class work. When we consider that these assigned novels may be the first they have ever read and the only novels they will read all year, we should not be surprised by this. In comparison to girls who have been reading novels for years, many boys have left themselves severely disadvantaged. Much of this chapter is aimed at how the reading reluctance of these a-literate teenagers can be managed and turned around. The general reasons for reluctance were outlined in chapter two, but here is a recap with specific reference to adolescents and high school.

High schools

The nature and organisation of high schools reflects the growing maturity of students and the expectations placed on them by staff. The students are not children any more; they are adolescents. They expect to be granted an increasing level of freedom, and in turn the school expects them to take more responsibility for themselves. Part of this expectation is that students manage across a range of subject areas without one teacher monitoring their progress on a daily basis, such as happens in primary school.

Homework increases also, and any reading component in this homework is likely to be assigned reading with an academic purpose — perhaps a literary novel the class is studying, some research for a humanities subject or a few pages from a science text book. While schools hope fervently that their students will read for pleasure, it is difficult to set aside periods in a crowded timetable even for lower secondary classes to do so. Among administrators, teachers who do not teach English and, for that matter, English teachers as well, there can exist a disappointing view that providing such reading periods is a waste of precious time.

The teacher librarian or English teacher may run a reading program such as R.I.B.I.T. (Read In Bed It's Terrific), but these are usually confined to the first year or two of high school. Unfortunately, such programs can sometimes reflect the enthusiasms of the teacher, so the lists of recommended material featured are predominantly, even exclusively, novels of approved literary worth. This relates to the civilising role that schools see themselves as having — a role I will address in more detail in the next chapter. But there is also another role that schools see themselves as having: to push, pressure, inspire, excite and ignite students towards the best academic results they can achieve. Some schools charge hefty fees for doing so. Reading for academic achievement is approved of. Reading to civilise is approved of. Reading for pleasure, where students are allowed to choose their own preferred reading material (which may well incur the disdain of teachers), is not particularly approved of, and may well be considered incompatible with the aims of the school.

The nature of adolescence

Adolescence is about defining your own identity as distinct from the forces that control your life and which you increasingly resent. (Schools and parents are the most prominent of these forces.) Adolescence is about deciding what you like and what you value, and finding ways to express these preferences. It is a difficult task,

and for boys a feature of this unsettling time can be a rejection of their earlier selves. Boys who were happy at primary school will suddenly tell you they hated it. The Year 6 teacher they once worshipped will now be shunned in the street or privately ridiculed by a group of former devotees. The boys know this is not quite right, but the pressure is on to be seen as a man, so childhood and childishness must be jettisoned. Books and the reading habit, especially the reading of children's novels, can be caught up in this and rejected along with the adolescent cringe towards their own former selves, which they are now embarrassed to recall.

The nature of adolescence is also exploited by the most unscrupulous marketing campaigns ever devised. The creators of such marketing regimes know all too well how intense is the need at this age to be identified with the right group. Certain material objects, certain behaviours and certain attitudes are 'cool'. Even those who are not entirely comfortable with them are even more uncomfortable if exposed with 'uncool' possessions, behaviour, attitudes or appearance. The irony is that in trying so hard to separate themselves from the tyranny of parents and school, teenagers submit themselves to the far more ferocious tyranny of their peers and brand names. (Only an adult can say this, and only to another adult. To teenagers such sentiments are proof that we do not understand!)

But we do understand, or at least we should understand this much — whether we like it or not, the novels and other reading material favoured by parents and teachers can seem decidedly 'uncool' as far as many teenagers are concerned. We keep telling the kids that it isn't so, or that it need not be so, yet they know conclusively that it just is. If we sit back and concede this as inevitable and intractable, nothing will change. But we don't have to accept defeat without a fight. The challenge is to see as many teenage boys as possible chanting: 'Reading rules! Books are cool!' High schools *can* achieve this. I have seen and heard of many successes. Such schools:

- provide scheduled reading periods, despite the crowded curriculum, thereby showing what an important activity reading (even for pleasure) is;
- allow regular visits to the library for classes, where the teacher and teacher librarian are active in recommending titles;
- provide adequate budgets for the purchase of a wide range of books and other reading material;
- encourage staff to read adolescent literature in order to better recommend titles to specific students;
- provide a welcoming and comfortable place for free reading periods;
- welcome students' choices (without comment or dissent) in free reading periods;

- nurture the expectation that every student, boy or girl, will be a reader.

A teacher from a regional grammar school told a recent conference that many boys joining his school from rural areas at Year 8 or Year 11 are amazed to encounter the firm expectation that they enjoy reading, and seem lost at first when set loose to find reading material to meet this expectation. Yet once the positive attitudes and practices of the school's approach begin to bite, they make this expectation their own, discover good books that they like, and settle into the reading habit.

Parents of a-literate teenage boys should look at the reading environment of their sons' schools and ask if there is a supportive attitude among teachers, particularly male teachers, and if there is an expectation that boys in the school will be readers. If so, are these expectations backed up by the practices noted above? The school environment is significant in building a culture of reading around boys, and if your son's school seems indifferent, bringing your concerns to the notice of decision makers is your right.

So much for school. What about the home? We know that, at fourteen, a boy is not as easily carried along by parental enthusiasm as he was at ten, especially where such enthusiasm runs counter to the behaviour demanded by his peer group. ('Wear a lycra shirt in the surf? Forget it, Mum! I'd look like a dag.') Here are some challenges for parents:

- Teenagers want to be taken seriously, so take their own reading seriously. Show an uncritical interest in it and welcome the discussion that might come forth from it.

- Teenagers want to be thought of as mature, so we should expect them to use reading to display their maturity. Challenge them to come up with a stand, complete with opinions which they can back up. Without embarrassing them or putting them on the spot, challenge them to support what they claim to believe. They will seek books and other reading material to achieve this. In turn, defend your position with reference to what you have read.

- Discussing events and issues in the home is an important support for reading. This resonates with the idea of reading for purpose. A boy will see that you, an adult, have drawn your firm and well-considered opinions not just from television or what you were taught at school twenty years before, but from newspapers and books, or the Internet. Even if they do not hurry off to read the same material in order to match you in argument, the framework is established in the mind of the teenager. Reading makes one stronger. Reading is power.

- Teenagers do not like instructions or dogmatic pronouncements, but they do seek and value guidance, especially of the informal variety. The books you keep in your house are part of that informal guidance, and they will have an influence on your son's development which may take twenty years for you to recognise. Such books say a great deal about you, and what you value and believe — and despite the angst of these years, your teenage sons do want to know what you believe and what you value. So be proud of your books and other reading material, select them carefully and keep them on show and available — and without ever pushing, recommend them when you think the time is right. They are needed.

Keep on ...

The positive practices of earlier years should continue.

- Keep up the encouragement, the interest and the easy display of affirmative attitudes towards reading.

- Keep up the purchase of books, visits to libraries (even if you are the one who goes and brings back piles of books) and the other strategies for surrounding your boy with material he might pick up and read at the most unpredictable times.

- Keep control over the TV, VCR and computer games.

- Be aware that holidays, particularly the long summer holiday, is when a boy has the most time on his hands.

Make sure books and other suitable reading material are available in abundance. Hit the library. Never go on holiday to the beach without a box of books.

An exception to every rule — the Bryce Courtenay syndrome

During my fifteen years as the librarian in an all-boys school, I sometimes came across a puzzling phenomenon. I dubbed it the Bryce Courtenay syndrome, and this is how it goes ...

For years, through middle and upper primary and on into the first year or two of secondary, teachers, librarians and parents encourage a boy to read. They offer him everything — fiction across all the genres, a wide range of non-fiction, cartoons and comic-style books, but to no avail. All such reading material is dismissed with contempt. A check of the boy's reading age shows him to be bobbing around the average for his class, yet still he complains that all books are too boring or too hard or too long, and he doesn't like reading, anyway.

Then, suddenly, when the boy is thirteen or fourteen, he is spotted in the playground with a copy of The Power of One or something similar tucked under his arm, a bookmark sprouting from page 451.

'You're not reading that,' the librarian challenges him. 'It's too hard, too long and you don't like reading, anyway.'

'No, it's great,' comes the reply, and the boy launches into an enthusiastic synopsis of the plot, confirming for

the incredulous librarian that he has read every word.

So what has happened here? I can only conclude that such boys simply did not like children's books or books written specifically for teenagers. There is no law that says you must. From earlier chapters, we know that boys find all manner of masculine models for themselves. These boys were not interested in identifying themselves among the young males of children's books. Not until they were introduced to popular adult fiction did they find satisfying story-lines and characters. I also suspect that such boys are harbouring latent reading skills that undergo a rapid growth spurt when finally confronted by something the boy truly wants to read.

Now before you turf out all your kids' books and guide your reluctant boy over to the adult shelves, this needs to be put into perspective. Most children find it enjoyable and appropriate to work their way through children's books, then teenage books, before moving on to adult material. Not every reluctant reader is hankering after The Power of One. *But for some, their reluctance is tied up with their self-image of a man in waiting for whom kid's stuff is beneath them even at ten years of age.*

List 9 comprises books you might recommend to your teenage son if he shows signs of the Bryce Courtenay syndrome. I suspect this syndrome is also related to the 'renegade reader' phenomenon discussed in chapter seven.

Years 11 and 12

Many secondary teachers will tell you that a lot of boys stop reading altogether in their final two years of school. Even good and willing readers may suddenly give away the habit. This is not so hard to understand when you consider that the academic results achieved at the end of Year 12 can determine a person's future. The pressure to stay focused on that final result is enormous. It is not reading as such which stops, because nearly all courses require reading to some extent. What can disappear is reading for pleasure. Sadly, reading anything that does not contribute to that all-important result can seem like an indulgence. But students who have learned to use reading as a welcome form of relaxation will not give away the habit. Not enough boys do learn this, though, and these are the ones who drift away from reading for pleasure in the crucial last years at school.

Don't panic if your son does seem to drift away. You have helped him acquire good reading attitudes and skills, so for now, be content that he is using these to achieve what matters most to him at this time. But since you have built a culture of reading around him throughout his formative and early teenage years, there is a strong chance that your son will come back to reading when the pressure is off. The first years after leaving high school are a wonderful time of freedom and discovery for a young man. Whether working or studying, there is more time to be himself and do what he really wants to do. Old peer groups break up, new friendships are made. Sporting interests become less intense and may fade as a means of supporting his self-esteem and masculine identity. His behaviour is no longer scrutinised on a daily basis by his school mates. This combination of new interests, a maturing self-awareness and the withering away of the reasons that rendered reading so unattractive can result in reading for pleasure being a pursuit he now takes up with delight. Unlike the teachers who wave goodbye to their students after Year 12 and may never hear from them again, your son will be with you for a few years yet. You, his parents, are the ones who will have the satisfaction of seeing your efforts produce a man who reads.

A personal account of how a reluctant boy became a man who reads

As a boy I was not a reader. I read Disney comics if one was lying around, or sporting magazines if a friend passed me one, but reading was never a first choice among my leisure activities. While I read the occasional novel, usually because the school required it, I was a slow reader and novels seemed tedious.

Two things nudged me into reading in my mid to late teens. In Years 11 and 12, my class studied William Golding's The Lord of the Flies, *still a favourite in schools thirty years later, and Graham Greene's* The Power and the Glory. *I adored both books. They were the first books I actually liked, the first that meant anything to me. They were not difficult* to read, and in discussing them — their themes, their symbolism and the intent of the author — I suddenly realised what a skill writing was, and that novels were more than just stories. The third book we studied was Thomas Hardy's Jude the Obscure. It proved impenetrable to me. I read it very slowly and found it very, very long. It is hardly surprising, then, that I hated both it and the idea of reading such long and difficult books.

The second nudge was holidays. Away from my friends, with plenty of time even after I had been for a swim, a fish and a wander around, I picked up the latest Reader's Digest condensed book which my parents had brought with us, and read a novel about a social worker living among the Kentucky Hillbillies. As soon as I had finished it, I started the next condensed story, about the survivors of an Andean plane crash. Both books fascinated me, so the experience was a pleasure. For the first time, I chose to read for pleasure, rather than do something active. After this, holidays became the time I read. The next Christmas, having finished Year 12, I read Something of Value by Robert Ruark and discovered yet again how much a novel could tell me about another land and another culture, and how much I could care about the characters. The book was two inches thick — much longer than Jude the Obscure. My aversion to long books disappeared.

Soon after, I came across East of Eden (John Steinbeck), read it slowly for the pure pleasure of the *saga, and wept on the last page* — *not just because the main character had died, but because there was no more of this wonderful story to read. I needed another book. Immediately. The first thing to hand was* The Return of the Native *by none other than Thomas Hardy. I was doubtful but desperate, so I read it. And loved it.*

I had become, and remain, a man who reads.
(Note — *I have since read most of Hardy, but not* Jude the Obscure. *Once bitten, twice shy! However, a school acquaintance who now reads the sports news on Channel 9 was asked to name his favourite novel for a celebrity feature in Brisbane's* Courier Mail. *He nominated* Jude the Obscure. *Who can tell which will be the books to confirm a young fellow's reading habit?)*

PART THREE

Reaching out to boys

CHAPTER SEVEN

Reaching out

I often hear the lament, 'Boys will be boys'. This chapter isn't about either confirming or challenging this statement. It is about accepting boys for who they are and what they like. At times, this means reaching out actively to boys *as they are*, rather than hanging back because they are not what we wish them to be. You should not despair if your son's reading tastes are not everything you would desire — at least he is enjoying books and reading. And besides, if you are prepared to lead the way, you can share the richness and rewards of literature with your son. Gradually, as he grows and matures, he will want to travel this path on his own.

What boys <u>do</u> like — a brave appraisal

To answer a question such as 'What *do* boys like to read?' is brave indeed — almost impossible, in fact. All manner of conflicting generalisations get in the way. For example, are we talking about willing readers or reluctant readers? Are we looking for books a boy will read by himself or books to read *to* a boy?

I will blaze ahead regardless with a few points distilled from my years as a teacher librarian in a boys' school.

- It is a mistake to believe that boys in general, and reluctant readers in particular, do not like fiction. It is often the type of fiction presented to them that is the source of their rejection. On the whole, boys enjoy books which place action ahead of emotion; what the characters *do* should be more important than what the characters think or feel. Hence the apparent preference for the action novel — the equivalent of thrillers and detective stories in adult reading matter. They often come in series to help with the marketing of them.

- Boys tend to like books which match their image of themselves. They want to be able to identify themselves and what they would like to be and do. This is why books about characters engaged in sport have always held at least an initial attraction for boys. Unfortunately, many novels with sporting action and themes fail because they do not deliver what the boy is expecting. This is often the unrealistic hope that reading the book will be just like playing the game. Sorry boys — no can do. There is a fundamental difference between doing something and reading about it. Other boys are lost when the story does not go where they want it to go; that is, in a direction close to their own personal experience. Few sport-centred novels live up to expectation.

- Boys love to have fun, so they want books that are fun — ones that make them laugh and appeal to their love of madcap mayhem. This is all tied up with their image of the quintessential boy, and as much as boyishness can be defined and replicated, they love to find it in the books they read. Few writers are able to capture that 'boyishness' in print. A significant part of the mayhem that boys love is poking fun at others, especially adults. Boys constantly find themselves being told to behave, to be tidier and less boisterous, so books where the characters triumphantly break free of these restrictions are greatly prized.

- Boys have an image of themselves as anarchic beings bringing chaos to stultifying order, even when they are the gentlest and most amenable lambs you could hope to have in the house. Used cynically, this can serve to reinforce the most destructive and dehumanising aspects of masculine stereotypes. Yet such cynicism badly misreads what boys are about. Yes, they love tales of subversion — but this subversion is oddly true to a sense of justice and what is right. Boys will grin and cheer when the villain comes to a sticky or humiliating end, but only when it is clear that such a fate is richly deserved.

Swashbuckler

I learned about boys' strong sense of justice first-hand after my short novel Swashbuckler *was released. I began to receive e-mails from children with a recurring complaint. During the story, two bullies who have threatened the main character suddenly find themselves implicated in the destruction of the school's rose garden. Though they are innocent, they have been cleverly framed to take the rap.*

My young readers were outraged by this injustice, even though the 'victims' were actually villains. I had to write a sequel, Buzzard Breath and Brains, *to satisfy this outcry for justice.*

Boyishness and good books

What is a good book for a boy?

You might well answer this way: a good book for a boy is one that takes him to places he has never imagined and shows him things that dazzle his mind. A good book challenges him to think about the world and his place in it. A good book stands firm in the face of the stereotypes that society presses on him, drawing out the emotional experience of his humanity which he might otherwise deny or repress. A good book is a rollicking yarn that tweaks his sense of adventure and absorbs him so completely that he battles alongside the hero and rejoices in the final victory as if it was his own. So much for fiction. Now for non-fiction. A good book for a boy is one that provides the information his thirsty mind seeks and inspires him to discover more. It fascinates him and opens up the possibilities of knowledge. It expands his world.

Stop! Let's get serious here. There are thousands of such books already in print and hundreds more published each year. Yet still reluctant boy readers are with us in grim battalions. To understand why, and to do something practical and effective about it, is the purpose of this book. So let's sweep away all the lyrical definitions of the good book that adults create and replace it with this simple statement: a good book for a boy is one he *wants* to read. The problem for many reluctant readers is that they are not being offered and encouraged to read the books and other reading material that they want to read. In short, the corner store is not stocking its shelves with what the customer wants to buy.

In chapter two I described how many boys are drawn into a masculine culture that is wary of books and reading. There is an underlying suspicion and discomfort, stemming from the association of a love for reading with the feminine and the 'school-approved', which they have learned to disdain. But the reverse is also true. Some women — and no small number of men — in the roles of teacher, librarian and parent can be suspicious and uncomfortable with boyishness. By this I am certainly not chanting 'boys will be boys' and defending oafish behaviour. By boyishness, I mean that innocuous immaturity best described by the old expression, 'frogs and snails and puppy dogs' tails'.

Boys love the ghoulish, the gross and the disgusting. Yet how often is this allowed to appear in children's books? When it does, it is carefully sanitised so as not to offend adult sensibilities. Almost every title that has ever attempted to make a story out of the messy, the uncouth and the horrible that so fascinates boys has attracted criticism or outright bans. Paul Jennings's stories were initially dismissed as toilet jokes.

Roald Dahl's *The Twits* was castigated for the nose-picking and other filthy habits portrayed. Raymond Briggs's *Fungus the Bogey Man* was banned in some American states, and a principal I once worked under tried to ban *How to Eat Fried Worms* simply because of the title. All of these books have achieved legendary status, especially among boys. They are all quite well written, while still managing to avoid sanitisation. Libraries and bookshops stock them with relish.

But there are many more books that fall outside the bounds of what is deemed worthy. Series horror in the vein of the *Goosebumps* phenomenon of the early 1990s are typical. These are formula stories, with quite ghastly and gory events described in their pages. Adults disdain them, even fear them. Yet such books have accomplished what many teachers, librarians and parents have tried to do but failed. They have found the right wavelength for boys. Boys actually want to read them.

The Place: *A Year 7 classroom. Boys only.*
The Time: *8.50 am*
The Scenario: *The teacher has been delayed in a parent interview. I am asked to take charge until he returns. Entering the room, what do I find? I find groups of enthusiastic boys in tight huddles, laughing, shouting, arguing — all in good spirits. I sidle up to see what all the fuss is about.*
They are swapping things among themselves, trading

*this one for that one. The room resounds with cries of
'No, I've had that one. Who's got number three? Come
on, let me have it.'*

*And what are they swapping? Basketball cards,
dodgy pictures? No. All this excitement centres around
a horror series known as* Fear Street *by R.L. Stine.*

• • •

*I have never seen a group of boys more excited by books
than these boys. They were not library books. The boys
had gone out and bought them with their own money,
dozens of them. It was completely separate from me and
remained so. Some would tell you this was a sad sight.
Such interest wasted on rubbish. I still think it was the
best thing I ever saw in all my years as a librarian.
These boys had built a culture of reading around
themselves. What made me sad was that the teacher
later banned such books and told the boys to read
something different, something better. They didn't.*

So here is a bit of heresy. The books we need — those
that will spark an interest in the reluctant reader — may
not be 'good' books at all but, on the contrary, books
that do not rate well on the criteria of literary merit.
Should we fret about this? No. A story is words on a
page. Reading it involves decoding those words to
make meaning. Perceptions of quality are judgments
applied arbitrarily. What adults value in a book is not
necessarily what boys value in a book. It doesn't have to
be the same, either, except in one vital aspect. If we are

to address reluctance to read, both adults and boys must value material that boys do want to read. Adults must be prepared to let boys walk in familiar territory before they are asked to run amid the richness that the wider adult world offers.

I am not saying here that we should immerse our boys in nothing but dross. I am saying that when we are encouraging boys to invest their time and effort in something they have so far seemed reluctant to do, we should consult them about what they might actually want to read. Then there is a chance they will see that, hey, reading is all right, reading is cool fun, reading can be full of the stuff that appeals to them, makes them laugh, makes them recoil with the cry, 'That's gross!' — and makes them quickly thrust the book under the nose of a mate with the words, 'Hey, you gotta read this.' This is how we build a culture of books and reading among our boys. As they mature towards manhood, their fascination for the ghoulish and disgusting will wane, but what will proceed into manhood with them is a culture of reading established and nourished through the years of boyhood.

Reluctance and the renegade reader

The conflict between boyishness and adult perceptions of good literature has produced an interesting pheno-menon which an American researcher, Jo Worthy, calls 'the Renegade Reader'.*

*' "On every page someone gets killed!" Book conversations you don't hear in school' *Journal of Adolescent and Adult Literacy* vol 41, 7, April 1998: pp. 508-516

I have encountered this phenomenon myself — along with its cousin, the Bryce Courtenay syndrome discussed in chapter six. The attitudes and habits of renegade readers, and the way adults view them, have a great deal to teach parents and teachers about the role of schools and how we might better foster a culture of reading around our boys within the school gate as well as outside it.

Renegade readers like to spend their free time playing sport and video games or 'hanging out' with their friends. However, they also read regularly. Their reading is made up mostly of comics, magazines, horror novels and suspense stories written for adults, plus a random assortment of non-fiction books about things that interest them. They are unconcerned by factors such as difficulty and length. In fact, the heftiness of a tome can be a status symbol for the boy who carries it.

They get hold of this reading material from their homes, their friends, the public library and from bookshops where they will spend their own money for an item they just have to have. (Can you pick the glaring omission from this list? That's right — no mention of the school library.)

In choosing a book, the big considerations for renegades are the genre, the author, the appeal of the title and the cover illustration, the blurb on the back and what their friends thought of it. The preferences of renegade readers can be quite narrow, even in a genre such as horror, where one author is 'hot' and another 'sux'.

A feature of renegade readers is their passion. They can become excited and very talkative about what they have read. When they share their reading experience with other boys there are no guidelines, no pre-set topics, no issues or skills to cover and no task to complete. Yet, research has found such informal discussions to include the language of book analysis which these same boys are loathe to produce in class for more literary works.

Renegade readers are the tragedy and the hope of reading reluctance among boys. They are regularly dismissed as reluctant by their teachers, and may similarly be labelled as such by their parents, who see, but do not recognise, the reading engaged in. These boys are *not* reluctant readers in the true sense. They are simply reluctant to read anything recommended by the school or anything that has a close association with school.

Renegade readers and the culture of schools

It is a tragedy that some boys who can and do read are turned off reading within the school environment. But the qualities many boys look for in reading material are very different from the qualities schools want their students to experience and appreciate.

If we just want boys to read, should we simply give them what they want and forget about the rest? No. There are good reasons why this cannot and will not happen. To understand why, we need to consider the role of the school in our society. This role has been established over many years — not just to teach basic skills, but to show young people what is worthy and valued by their society. It is expected that schools promote the highest standards in all fields and produce students who aspire towards those standards. In other words, schools are a civilising force within society. This is nowhere more evident than in the kinds of reading material that schools lay before students, both for study and as recommended reading for pleasure. Such reading is seen as having a civilising influence.

Schools have a commitment to literary quality. They buy books for the library and the classroom to support this commitment. They encourage the reading of high-quality material to promote the features of good writing which students should recognise and try their best to emulate. If there were no such books in the school, and if students were not encouraged to read this literature, the school would be failing in its important social and cultural role.

But renegade readers won't touch it with a barge pole, and neither will boys with poor reading skills and a hardening reluctance to read anything at all. Worse still, these reluctant boys come to resent school reading as an imposition on them. Renegades consider it inconvenient and, most telling of all, something that gets in the way of the personal reading they do enjoy. Parents and teachers should take note of what one commentator had to say about this: 'We need to value and legitimate what students do outside school rather than bemoan what they are not reading in school.'*

*W.P. Bintz, 'Resistant readers in secondary education: Some insights and implications' *Journal of Reading* vol 36, 1993: p. 614

*After I had given an address at a recent conference where I mentioned renegade readers and the role of schools, a member of the audience suggested it was essential that books have a civilising influence on students. His argument was that there was nothing else left in the curriculum which could perform this role. After all, how many students still studied history or civics? Humanities subjects are rapidly being replaced by vocational courses in our high schools.*

I could not disagree with the man. However, I feel it is putting unrealistic expectations on the study of literature that it be the only way still left to us to civilise our boys. Renegade readers show us that in using literature so blatantly and desperately for this purpose, we risk driving reading for pleasure 'underground'.

Two kinds of book

To build a culture of reading around our boys, then, we need to recognise the difference between:

- books for reading *to* reluctant boys, and
- books for reading *by* reluctant boys.

This difference is significant in developing a connection between boys and books. It is the difference between books a boy will enjoy reading by himself, and books a boy will enjoy only when adults read them to him. This is particularly important when boys are in middle and upper primary school. Adults who have never been reluctant readers cannot recall a time when reading was anything other than easy and a pleasure. Such adults need to understand this difference.

There are a number of factors involved. When reading is the job of someone else, the difficulty and, in particular, the length do not deter a reluctant reader. Two hundred, three hundred pages — it doesn't matter as long as it is a great story. New words and sophisticated sentence structures are no problem because the adult will smooth the way towards meaning.

When it comes to the content of a book, there is an unconscious understanding between adults and boys about what is expected and acceptable. For example, boys enjoy swearing like bullock drivers among themselves, but never dare so much as a 'bloody' in front of an adult. So it is with books. It is difficult to persuade boys to read books which focus on emotional experience as well as physical experience. But when an adult does the reading, both the adult and the boy can explore the emotional experience of characters together. It is here boys learn that these elements are essential and valuable parts of the story rather than an interruption to the swift flow of events, and since someone else is doing the reading, they accept it (and even take an understated interest in it). Robert Newton Peck's *A Day No Pigs Would Die* is about the son of a dying pig farmer, and is set in a strict religious community in Vermont. As a book for reluctant readers to try on their own, it would not be at the top of my list. The setting is a culture many boys would find 'weird', some of the colloquial dialogue is difficult to interpret, and at times in this 180-page book the relationships of the characters take precedence over what is happening. These are not qualities that normally entice reluctant male readers.

But if you should read this novel to your son, a few chapters each night, both you and he will become immersed in the day-to-day struggle of a family you will care deeply about. At the end, you may well weep together for the sadness and the joy the book gives you. What a human experience to share with your son. What a literary experience to encourage his interest in books and deepen his understanding of what a story can do.

There are thousands of such books (a good selection appears in List 7). Good and willing readers tackle them on their own. Unfortunately, for reasons of masculine self-image, content and difficulty, reluctant readers will rarely do so. Yet all boys should gain access to these stories. They do love them, even if some may not feel able to tell you so. They serve a vital linguistic purpose, also. A boy will find it much easier to read challenging works when he has heard more sophisticated sentence structures read to him and been introduced to a far wider vocabulary by such reading.

 *The concept of reading aloud to an adult or even a twelve year old seems foreign to us. Yet until little more than a century ago, this was the norm. Shakespeare and other playwrights never intended their plays to be read in classrooms or studied as texts. They wanted them to be experienced in a theatre. Poets expected their work to be read aloud to a group and shared. Modern poets still do. Most novels written before the mid-nineteenth century were shared in the same oral manner, as the majority of the population could not read before this time. A literate person in the household was the equivalent of the modern radio — an entertaining voice — and the book was the raw material. Even after literacy became common, families still read to one another.*

So consider both kinds of book for your son. If he finds his boyishness identified and celebrated in the books he reads for himself, he will read them happily, and books will become a part of his life. His reading skills are constantly practised and improved, even though the quality of what he reads may not always meet with the approval of some. Meanwhile, continue to read good books to him at home. When the day comes for him to say, 'Mum (or Dad), I don't want you to read to me any more,' it will be because he is already reading books of similar calibre for himself. He will read such books, the type suggested in Lists 8 and 9 on pages 207 to 213, because his immaturity is falling away and he wants something more than mere boyishness in the books he reads for himself. He will read these books because he is comfortable with the culture of reading that has been built around him.

Books not to read to your boys

There are certain books that you should not read to your son in the usual fashion where you read and he listens. Ideally, you should leave them for your boy to read on his own. These are those all-too-rare books that meet the content and difficulty requirements of reluctant boys. List 10 (on page 213) sets out such books, with names like Dahl and Jennings prominent. I wish it was ten pages long. Encourage your son to read these books, or perhaps you could read the first chapter or two aloud — but since he is capable of reading them on his own (and more than likely tempted to), don't do it all for him.

This is not a hard and fast rule. Sometimes he might come to you and say, 'I just read this. It was fantastic! Will you read it to me?' Do it for the fun of sharing and reinforcing his enthusiasm. The reverse is not uncommon either. If you do choose to read a book of this type to him, he will go off and read it all again on his own, and enjoy it just as much. Since some of the writers on the list have several titles, you might read

one as a way of encouraging your son to attempt
the others. *

But the basic principle remains. These books are
over to him, to read on his own. For these are the books
that will take your son's fledgling reading skills and
hammer them into the confidence and fluency that can
tackle anything.

*The list is by no means exhaustive. Your intimate
knowledge of boyishness might lead you to books I
have never heard of. (If so, please drop me a postcard
detailing the author and title. I collect such titles. They
are more precious than gold.)

CHAPTER EIGHT

Books and beyond: reading material for boys

In the last chapter, I argued that we should accept our sons' boyishness and encourage them to read what they *want* to read as well as what we think they *should* read. The important thing is that they read. I would like to expand on that in this chapter by discussing in more depth the type of reading material that appeals to boys — and some strategies for encouraging them to read it.

Using the nature of boys

Competitiveness and rewards

Masculine culture is often a competitive culture, so efforts can be heightened and sustained by the promise of reward. The kind of competitiveness I am going to suggest here pits the boy against himself — or, in effect, his own reluctance to read. There are only winners in this contest.

There are any number of ways to spur on a boy's reading through competitiveness, and any number of rewards to offer. Being boys, chocolate bars and ice-creams will no doubt feature highly among the young. The older the boys get, the more mature the rewards — cinema tickets perhaps. I have even heard of parents paying their children to read. It beats washing the car to earn pocket money, and the benefits outweigh sparkling paint work.

Boys love to check their progress, too, and take pride in what they achieve. A chart on the fridge or the bedroom door will serve as both a reminder and further incentive as he sees himself inching closer to a goal.

As far as possible, let him choose books and other reading matter for himself. If it seems to be all the same, negotiate some adjustments to the rules — but do your best to maintain the spirit of fun. No matter what the reward, if the whole exercise is a boring trial for your son, he will not respond.

Rewards and incentives are frowned on by some. It is true that when the incentives cease, the reading usually drops away again. But they have positive features well worth the effort.

- For a while at least, a boy is enthusiastic about books.
- Reading skills are enhanced willingly.
- A range of books he would otherwise not have read become part of his experience.

- There is a chance of discovering that 'special book' which opens him up to reading's fun and purpose, and sets him on the path of lifelong enthusiasm.

A great way to encourage variety and fun within a competition is to stage a reading Olympics with different events. Boys can earn gold, silver or bronze in events such as reading funny poems to the family at dinner, finding five interesting facts in an information book, reading a sci-fi novel or a mystery, or for undertaking a reading marathon (ie two hours non-stop).

Be aware, too, of what is happening at school. Many primary teachers place reading expectations on boys, involving so much reading per night and record keeping to show that it is done. In secondary, it might be the teacher librarian who runs a R.I.B.I.T. (Read In Bed It's Terrific) program, also requiring lists and signatures. In this case, parents should work together with the school's program, offering encouragement, interest, approval and, of course, rewards for good performance.

Peer groups and fads

By the time a boy is in upper primary school, and certainly through secondary school, the opinions, attitudes and actions of his peer group are as important, if not more important, to his self-image and well-being as his family. Can the peer group be used to help build a culture of reading? I think it can be, though a little subtlety is required and the limitations of parental input firmly understood.

Parental interference in a boy's choice of friends is not welcome, and any 'suggestions' or other attempts to influence behaviour are not valued. Realistically, masculine peer groups are unlikely to be energised by or centred around books and reading (though I have seen it happen). One approach you might take is to accept that your son's peer group is anti-literacy (or sees itself that way) and provide a counterbalance in the home. A boy whose friends don't read, or who are disparaging about those who do, can still be a reader at home if the books, the right place, the time in the day, and your encouragement and approval are all there in support. I hope you provide this anyway. But do not despair of masculine peer groups where the boys appear reluctant to read. A culture of reading can be supported by reading matter that is valued by the culture of these groups — like magazines, comics, books on sport and some websites.

Fads, fashions, trends — whatever you want to call them — can sweep through a group, and the group's obsession becomes the focus of individuals, even if it is an unfamiliar behaviour. These provide a great opportunity for the clever parent. It is important to support this where it happens by supplying the books/materials. It is even more important not to take it over, because then it becomes a behaviour imposed from outside, from among the adults. Where part of the group identity is rebelling against adults and the adult-approved, such behaviour would immediately lose its appeal.

Support can be given through a group member; for parents, this means your own son. Material presented to him on the basis that maybe his friends would like it, since they seem so interested, has a chance. Furthermore, your son has a way of enhancing his position in the group by introducing a valued extension of the current obsession. The group benefits by finding a new way to experience and enjoy the focus of their attention. The culture of reading among those boys is enhanced by having a common interest associated with reading and because, at least for a while, the disapproval of reading as a behaviour has been relaxed.

Be warned — it will cost you, and the group's boyishness is unlikely to see any magazine, comic or book you post into this opportunity treated with the respect you might feel it deserves. It will get kicked, torn, trodden on etc. But remember that the aim is to see the item read and valued for what is in it, not revered as an artefact. If this is achieved, does it matter what condition the item itself is in afterwards? What this might also cost you is that position of control over what is read, when and how it is read, and the very purpose for the reading.

The right book

One of the joys of being a teacher librarian is to see a reluctant reader blossom into a happy and willing one. It does happen. Sometimes, it is one book that does the trick. (See the Bryce Courtenay syndrome in chapter six.) It is finding that one book that takes time. As singer Don McLean once said, 'I worked hard for ten long years until a record company gave me a break. Then the newspapers called me an overnight success.' The right book can be that 'overnight success' which is in fact the pay-off for years of trying.

It is impossible to predict with any confidence what will be the right book for any particular boy. The personal interests that connect with that book can lie hidden, even from the boy himself. Love for a book may develop because the book was shared with a special adult. Equally, its significance can come from the very fact that it was read alone. For another boy, it might be more a question of the right time, coinciding with a shift in his maturity; the same book, if attempted six months before, would have been rejected, yet with his growing insight and thirst for new things the book now strikes a chord.

The right book is one that allows a boy to discover reading and what books have to offer in a personal way. It ceases to be something that adults keep nudging him towards and becomes something he chooses for himself. It marks the end of reluctance. Afterwards, he goes searching for books that take him to the same heights of adventure, emotional engagement, personal identity, or whatever it was in that special book that stirred him. The job then is to keep the books flowing through to him so that the positive experience is confirmed and repeated. To give your son a chance of finding the 'right book' to set him on his way, he needs books at hand, and he needs books continually brought to his attention.

Difficulty and length

If a boy is going to read a book himself, then the book must match his reading ability. Obviously, if it is too hard, the effort of decoding the words and making meaning will result in the story being lost in a sea of confusion and frustration. It is akin to the layman trying to make sense of an old-style legal document. (Whereas the party of the first part, hereafter known as the plaintiff ...) Who would go on in such circumstances if the object was pleasure? Certainly not me!

When they can be convinced to read a story, reluctant boys read for the interest and entertainment the book brings them. All other considerations are secondary. But reluctant readers are often slow readers, for whom reading involves significant effort. If the novel takes its time with the story, then no matter how brilliant the language or characterisation, the flow of events is simply too slow in coming. This creates another kind of difficulty. The boys do not get sufficient reward for their effort. Boys whose reluctance is related to indifferent reading skills will baulk at long books for this reason. They want reward for effort. What's more, they should get it!

Some technical details to consider

- The design of a book is important. The layout of the page needs to be open, with plenty of white space. This is often a failing with inexpensive books which have sacrificed these important factors in order to keep costs down.

• The typeface needs to be appropriate to the boy's age group and reading ability. Too small and the book will seem too hard. Too large or exotic may suggest a book for babies, which risks insulting him. If tentative reading skills are a factor in his reluctance, he does not need to be reminded that he is on a par with much younger children.

• Short chapters help. This hints at a fast-moving story, and allows the boy to feel he is getting into it, gaining visible reward for his efforts by mowing down the chapters. Boys like to feel a sense of achievement in whatever they do and milestones like chapter headings provide this.

• Covers make a difference. No girls, please, though canny librarians have long discovered that a boy can often be talked into a book with a girl on the cover as long as his friends are not standing around. The cover is also intended to be a guide towards the contents. Wacky cover illustration means wacky story. Kids don't need to be told this — and, unlike the wise old saying, they certainly *do* judge a book by its cover.

Parents need to know these things. Even though they will probably never oversee the creation of a book, it is certainly part of their role to select books to bring into the house. As I have emphasised before, this is a vital part of creating a reading environment, of surrounding your son with print and opportunities to read. So if you are choosing a book in a bookshop, or a dozen from the library to supplement his own wary choices, keep these details in mind.

Facts and figures and doing things

It has long been observed that many boys are attracted to non-fiction books, or, as we call them now, information books. The trick is to use this to help create a reading culture and expand outwards from there into broader reading interests.

In general, it is certainly true that boys are drawn to books with facts, figures and information. Such books match their image of themselves as male. A boy sees it as his role, far more than a girl's, to collect information about 'things' and appear knowledgeable, thereby confirming his mastery of himself and his world. Boys do not normally read for detailed information about a single topic. This is not part of a child's nature anyway.

Sometimes, the attraction is spurred by a personal interest, a popular movie or an event such as the Olympics. But on the whole, boys use non-fiction books in a random fashion prompted by no more than a fascination for information and detail. To a boy, information is fun, and bears no relation to detailed analysis or structured learning. It is not surprising, then, that girls easily outshine them in school research activities. This, though, is a function of literacy skills and attitude to school work. The information books boys prefer are rarely useful for the type of research that teachers require.

The books that fascinate boys present information in 'bite-sized' grabs. Easily understood and recalled,

these are often of an amazing or statistical nature, with little connection beyond a link to a common theme. Boys browse through these information books, dipping in wherever the mood takes them. Large dollops of text are left unread. The publishers of children's information books have come to recognise this in recent years, and have responded by keeping text to a minimum. Design and illustration have improved dramatically too. Take a look at what is available in the *Cross-Section* books by Stephen Biesty and the Dorling Kindersley Eyewitness Guides. That is why it is important to seek out the best. Coffee-table style adult books can hold a fascination for boys because of the exquisite photographs, but pages filled with text will not even be glanced at.

Boys linger over illustrations, the more detailed the better. Browsing is often a shared activity, even up to Years 6 and 7, and should be recognised and respected as such. The fascination a boy feels for the snippets of information he is collecting at times demands sharing. That sharing may be done with you around. Listen to him. He is telling you that he can read and does read and, what's more, is excited by what he is reading.

But is browsing, studying illustrations and largely ignoring the text, really reading? It is not sustained reading in the sense of reading a novel — and without sustained reading, fluency cannot develop. However, browsing through facts, figures and information contributes to visual literacy, which is vital as well. The aim is balance. To immerse a boy in nothing but information books risks leaving him a walking encyclo-paedia of trivia who cannot make sense of an eight-line paragraph. Nor will it work if you deliberately choose books for him that steer him down a narrow path.

Information is fun, but it is by no means frivolous. Interests sparked by non-fiction books early on can lead to lifelong passions and hobbies, and may well influence career choices. As ever, though, a boy is walking the tightrope of behavioural expectations. The choice of what he is interested in, the type of book he expresses that interest through, and the way he shares and demonstrates his mastery of the information acquired, governs whether he is labelled 'cool' or the complete opposite, 'a nerd'.

Books in series

Boys like books in series. In recent years, it has become common for such series to be numbered. There is something about this ploy that appeals to boys in the same way that numbered sporting cards were once collected. Perhaps it is that very collectability, the urge to 'own' a full set, which works to the advantage of literacy. (Of course, with friends interested in the same books — and let's not forget libraries — owning them is not essential.) Sharing series books around among the peer group is part of the attraction, too, allowing boys to gain kudos for having read more, or having the latest or most difficult title to get hold of.

All this will hardly be news to many adult men. The famous Biggles books from decades ago were not numbered, but were certainly read in numbers. There is something about the comfortable familiarity of the characters. Such books are usually plot-focused anyway. Many great writers list series books as an obsession of their youth that contributed greatly to their love of reading and their subsequent writing careers. Not a bad recommendation!

Though series books are sometimes criticised for the predictable nature of the stories and the sense of sameness about them, these qualities are in fact what makes them so appealing. When a boy chooses a book, his first question is not: 'Is this a book of sound literary quality?' Boys never ask this question; neither do girls or adults very often, if the truth be known. The only question considered is this: 'Will I like this book?' If he has already read and enjoyed a book in the same series, he knows there is a good chance he will like it. Adults do exactly the same. They discover one book they like and quickly read three or four others by the same author, often with the same central character. We should be fair and let boys make this one of their reading habits as well. Not all numbered series fall foul of the more literary-minded either. The *After Dark* series was written by some of the most prominent names in Australian literature.

Getting your son hooked on a series may see him rattle through four or five books before the appeal wears off. His hunger for them will leave television and video games ignored for as long as it lasts. With continuous series — which should really be called serials, because each book is an instalment of a larger story — the readers can become fanatical about acquiring and reading each new book as it appears. Where is the reading reluctance here? John Marsden's series, beginning with *Tomorrow When the War Began*, is a prime example. The Harry Potter books are another.

Series books keep the reading happening. They are not always particularly challenging but this doesn't matter. They are fun. They help a boy get a feel for reading as a pleasurable part of his life. They contribute to the fluency that will help boys tackle more literary works when they have to.

Series are not confined to fiction, either. Many wonderful series of information books have appeared in the last fifteen years. The prices are often high, and owning an entire series would break the bank, but knowing that there is a range of books of this type in existence will send boys off to find them in libraries. (See List 12 for suggestions.)

Another medium that appears in numbered series is comic books. The Asterix and TinTin series (the only comic books deemed 'acceptable' by most school libraries) may not be numbered, but each one has the rest of the series cleverly set out on the back cover, and I have seen boys make their way through one after the other, happily swapping them between friends until they have read the lot. I kept photocopies of the back cover handy for kids who wanted to keep track of what they had and hadn't read.

Magazines

Magazines can play an important role in the reading habit of boys through late primary and early secondary school. They are usually welcomed by teenage boys in a way that novels and other books aren't. Some are unmitigated rubbish, it must be said, but this is by no means the case for all magazines. They deserve consideration as a plank in that culture of reading we are trying to build and maintain around our boys.

The great appeal, and therefore the significant advantage, that magazines have is that they cover topics of intense interest to boys at this age, and they are presented in a way that matches closely the trends of the day. Topics range from surfing, cars and motorbikes to computers, video games, popular music and, depending on the season, a wide range of sports.

To get hold of magazines, boys (or their parents) must either buy them or borrow them from libraries. Don't forget the latter. In fact, browsing through the range of titles stocked by the library can be a good way of discovering which magazines interest a boy most.

The widest range, though, is likely to be found at the newsagency. Comparing a range of titles concerned with the same topic is best done here. Unlike library copies, these magazines are not free — but if you can afford to buy the magazine, the added advantages of ownership will follow:

- using the magazine to build status among a peer group;
- having the magazine available at all times;
- taking personal pride in it;
- watching a collection grow on a bedroom shelf.

When a particular magazine does take your son's fancy, consider subscribing to it. The day it arrives, he will disappear into his room until teatime. Your son is a willing reader.

If you are still wary of magazines, worried that they are not legitimate reading material and that they may hinder rather than sustain a culture of reading, consider these points:

- Magazines can be a source of information about other literature and an encouragement for boys to pursue it. Technical books, biographies and even novels related to the subject matter are often discussed, featured or reviewed and offered as prizes.
- Magazines can be a focus for developing critical and visual literacy skills in an enjoyable and interesting way for boys who are so alienated from the texts offered to them at school that they never learn these skills.
- Magazines are an important source of that eclectic browsing for random scraps of information that can actually give boys an advantage over girls who stick exclusively to novels.
- Enjoying one type of magazine can lead a boy on to others, expanding his world of print and what he gets from it. Such

expansion may even spark that personal interest which leads to a satisfying career in the years ahead.

- Reading and browsing through magazines can maintain literacy skills, particularly the speed and level of comprehension which requires regular practice.

 *At one high school I know of in Queensland, a teacher discovered that every second Thursday he had difficulty getting the attention of the boys in his science class. A little investigation revealed that, under their desks, they were busy perusing the new edition of the* Trading Post. *This was a serious business, looking for car parts and the other paraphernalia that interested the boys.*

Rather than act against it, the teacher has since made it part of the lesson, allowing discussion of the various items — which are overpriced, which form of words sounds like a smokescreen for a poor quality item …? He understands that what he has going in that classroom is practical, critical literacy. No one is reluctant to read during these classes.

Comics

If noses begin to wrinkle when magazines are mentioned, nostrils positively flare if the word 'comics' is so much as whispered. But it is a mistake to dismiss comics altogether as unworthy and unsuitable reading matter for boys. Research has shown that reading comics does not replace other kinds of reading. In fact, boys who read comic books tend to read just as much non-comic material, and there is evidence that many read much more. Comic books are centred not only within the popular culture of boys, but they closely resemble the conversational style of language boys use in the schoolyard and among friends. School language — the language of the classroom — is more academic and formal in style. Comics can help to bridge the gap between the two.

Contrary to popular belief, comic books often embrace a wide vocabulary and introduce unusual words, at times playing with language, which is a great thing for children to experience. At the very least, they add to the print environment that parents should seek to build around boys. Some comics in the Marvel Superhero range delve extensively into mythology and obscure branches of science which can spur a boy's interest and lead on to reading of greater depth.

My own brother was a comic fanatic from his late primary years. At the time he read little else, and he will not mind me saying that he was an indifferent scholar. His favourite comics were the Marvel Superhero series featuring the Norse gods Thor, Woden, Loki and others. He collected those comics with a

religious fervour and his knowledge of Norse mythology, while not terribly academic, was certainly extensive.

Then a friend told him about Tolkien. Overnight, he went from reading comics to The Lord of the Rings. *That was just the start. Fantasy, sci-fi — even classics such as Hardy's* Return of the Native. *It was the copy he bought in a second-hand bookshop which I read during my own reading epiphany. By then, my brother was a frequent visitor to second-hand bookshops.*

It all started with those comics. Today his valuable collection is kept under lock and key. The rest of his house bulges with books.

To many boys, reading is not associated with fun. Comics are fun. Boys who read a lot of comic material read more often for pleasure. They associate reading comic books with enjoyment and, best of all, boys who read more comics than their friends also read more books for pleasure and have more positive attitudes towards reading. While Archie and Disney comics have a reading level of around Year 2, superhero and other comics of this type fall between Years 4 and 6 in reading level. They do contribute towards the improvement of reading skills, and they do help boys to read more difficult material.

Perhaps comics are not quality literature. No one is going to tear a novel from a boy's hand to replace it with a comic. But the evidence does not support the scorn that teachers and other adults pour on comics.

Banning them or disparaging them denies boys the benefits they offer and adds further to the perception that reading is not allowed to be fun, that it is a 'school' thing with no relevance to life beyond the school gate.

Another view of television and movies

Many of the movies and television programs heavily geared towards children are accompanied by a range of merchandise. A favourite tie-in is the novelisation of the story, while the more enterprising publishers even produce non-fiction books as well, dealing with the production of the movie or information about special effects or the movie's wider imaginative environment.

Books can then become part of the excitement generated by these movies and the marketing campaigns that support them. The novelisations, while not great literature, carry with them their own motivation to read the book to the end, therefore helping to build the fluency boys need. I saw this plainly with my own eight-year-old son. The first book of any length he read cover-to-cover was a junior version of The Phantom Menace. *He sat on his bed for two days, jumping off occasionally to have a few words explained by Mum or Dad. Only his fascination with the movie sustained him through this difficult task. Afterwards, the pride in his achievement was visible in his face. The value to his self-image and confidence as a reader was priceless. Within weeks, he was tackling much more challenging and literary material without concern.*

(Note — his parents quietly put that better quality reading in his way ...)

Computers and the Internet

Young people, especially boys, have taken to computers as though the world was never without them. There are even computer programs designed to help develop reading skills, and many students will have already encountered these. Certainly, if a reading exercise involves the use of a computer, reading reluctance among boys is reduced.

But these reading development programs are not what boys in upper primary and secondary school rush to the computer to enjoy. Most commercial computer games are a dead loss for building or maintaining reading skills. A few, like 'Where in the world is Carmen Sandiego?', manage to make at least some reading integral to the game without losing their appeal, though I note with sadness that as computers become more powerful and use more multimedia, video and audio presentations have replaced text as a way of delivering crucial information needed for the game.

The Internet can seem like a dead loss as well, particularly if a boy is simply browsing from site to site, clicking on whatever pictures look interesting. He might not have much idea of what kind of site he is going to, and will navigate for long periods, largely ignoring any text he sees. But don't dismiss the Internet as a source of reading material. Formal and focused learning through the Internet does not get far without reading. It is increasingly used in research activities, even with quite young children, and these activities can be extended in the home as well. E-mail also involves reading. The evidence shows that boys like to communicate with each other in this way, and even if few e-mails seem to extend beyond a couple of lines, it is still an effective reinforcement of skill and purpose.

The Internet will not kill reading. It should be seen more as a fabulous communication tool which will make the ability to read and a willingness to read even more essential in the future. In as much as boys are drawn to computers and the Internet, it has the capacity to cut through the reluctance to read that troubles so many boys and so we should encourage them (and their sisters) to use it to its fullest extent for learning and for pleasure, even if we sometimes question whether any reading is taking place at all.

Beyond books

I hope by now I have shown — as I have been attempting to do throughout *Boys and Books* — that not all worthwhile reading is found in books. Indeed, to confine a boy's reading to nothing but books would do him a disservice. So we should surround boys with a variety of reading material, some of it challenging and some of it simply fun. And we should encourage them in the ways that boys like to be encouraged until reading becomes an enjoyable and permanent habit, and reading skills are built and maintained.

CHAPTER NINE

A note to fathers (and other male role models)

Here is a question for the fathers of sons, and for those men who find themselves acting as a role model for boys:

Do you want your boys to make books and reading a part of their lives?

Presumably, if you are reading this book, it is something you consider important, and so the answer is yes. You may have a son too young for formal reading, yet you want to know how best to guide him. You may have noted that the nine-year-old son of your new partner is showing a reluctance to read anything much at all and feel a sense of disquiet. This cannot be a good thing, you say to yourself. There could be trouble ahead if that attitude persists. Whether I am his father or not, I play a special role in his life. I have a responsibility. And so you do. Infant or young tearaway, you care for him. You want him to do well in life and you want him to be happy. You know only too well from your own experience that he is unlikely to be happy if he does not do well in the things he turns his hand to. This applies equally whether he becomes a barrister before the High Court or a brickie's labourer.

Chapter one sets out why boys need books and reading — for their schooling, employment prospects and civic participation, but also for the not so easily measured benefits of understanding other people and the nourishment of their souls. These may well contribute more to a person's well-being than the purely functional reasons listed first.

In contemporary Australian society, the task of teaching boys the skill of reading, and then encouraging them to use it, has largely fallen to women — primary school teachers, teacher librarians and public librarians (most in these three professions being women), mothers and secondary English teachers. (There are more female English teachers in schools than female maths/science teachers.) In chapter two I discussed how this contributes to stereotyped attitudes about reading as a feminine activity that can contribute to reading reluctance in boys.

It is time men stepped up to play their vital role in developing boys' reading skills. If we want a culture of reading built around our boys, then a man's got to do what a man's got to do ...

Attitude

In the chapters of part two I emphasised the importance of parents maintaining and modelling positive attitudes towards reading. The evidence is clear on this point. A number of research projects have found that the example set by a father who reads is not as potent as commonsense would suggest. Fathers who read a great deal do not automatically produce sons who do the same. Nor do fathers who describe themselves as indifferent necessarily produce reluctant readers. The telling factor in this research was found to be whether books and reading were actively valued in the household. Attitude! The attitude of a boy's father towards reading has a far greater influence than the attitudes modelled in schools.

Young boys take their early attitudes towards almost everything from within their home environment. They learn what to value by observing what family members — parents in particular — say and do, and how they interact with the wider world. There is no questioning or critical appraisal at this stage. Boys take it for granted that these attitudes are good and right, and they are very hard to break. As the strongest model of masculine attitudes, the father has an enormous and longstanding influence on his sons. Even when a boy passes through a rebellious adolescence, at times disowning his father altogether, basic attitudes learned from Dad — towards women, towards violent behaviour, towards authority — are retained with little change. The Jesuits knew this when they coined that infamous line, 'Give me a boy to the age of seven and I will give you the man.'

Attitudes to books and reading are no different.

Let's assume that you value reading very highly and you want your son to do the same. You are unlikely to hand your three year old a signed declaration of these values, nor are you going to sit down with a seven year old and have a man-to-man talk about it all. Instead, everything you say and do in relation to books and reading will become a brick in the construction of your son's attitude towards them. Up to his teenage years, he very much wants to be like his dad, so you are watched closely and listened to, even when you are unaware of it. I am sorry if this has you glancing over your shoulder, wary of Big Brother and the thought police! But the point must be made. It is easy to be drawn into saying or doing something that aligns you with a stereotype, even when that stereotype does not represent your personal values. Sad as it is, the predominant masculine culture that will envelop your son as he gradually becomes independent assigns little worth to reading. Fathers need to prepare their sons for this by passing on attitudes that value reading in the home. All that is really needed is a subtle awareness of your own casual comments and actions — what you might call Dad's whispers. To a boy, they sound like shouts. Every word that boosts reading builds a positive attitude and every word that disparages it, even those said in jest, kick those positive attitudes into the dust.

Don't forget example

Despite the promotion of attitude over example made earlier, example is still a powerful way of showing what you value without saying a word.

Here are a few points to consider.

- You may well read extensively, but only in bed after your son has gone to sleep. Does he ever see you reading? Often, it is enough for him to see a book open on its belly beside your bed, but a casual reference helps confirm the matter. 'Careful you don't tread on my book there. I'm really enjoying it.'

- Not all fathers are novel readers, and you don't need to pretend for your son's sake. The aim here is wide-ranging reading, and by no means are all great books novels. For that matter, not all great reading matter is found in books. Magazines and newspapers are important as well, especially where they support a personal interest your son already knows you have.

- While the image of the father ignoring his family as he peruses the morning paper is not one to cultivate, it is a valuable demonstration of reading. Later, it can move into shared reading of the sports, entertainment or features pages. Of course, eventually your son might pinch the sports pages from under your nose — but as you curse him, be comforted by the sight of a boy who has made meaningful and enjoyable reading part of his daily routine.

- Whatever you read, and whether it happens on a weekday morning or Sunday afternoon, a significant element of the example you set comes from the incidental comments and discussions that

occasionally stem from it. Sometimes these might be directed at your wife or daughter, but your son will take note. Draw him in as well if you find something to share with him. It might be a picture, or an amazing fact that will appeal to him. By not only seeing you read but hearing you share what it brings you, your example shows him that reading is interesting, useful, enjoyable and very much a part of your life as a man.

Enthusiasm and encouragement

This heading seems self-explanatory, perhaps, and one might well argue that enthusiasm and encouragement are simply extensions of attitude in any case. Yet there is a subtle difference that earns them a separate mention. While values and attitudes are passed from father to son in myriad unseen ways, to show enthusiasm and offer encouragement are more conscious acts, undertaken with a deliberate purpose in mind.

A father's enthusiasm has enormous potential

to motivate his son. It is the father's manner of speaking and his eagerness to see his son have a go that makes a boy want to take part, whether the activity is football, swinging on an old tyre or getting stuck into some reading. Encouragement gives that enthusiasm practical effect. Boys will take on a great deal to please their dad. When it is clear that a man wants his son involved in an activity, and the reward is the approval of the most significant man in his life, the incentive is sky high to give it a go. This gives you enormous power to guide your son. Some of that power, at least, can be spared to guide him towards books and reading.

Involvement and commitment

So far, I have encouraged fathers and other male role models to comment on what they are reading in order to show that reading offers interest, information and fun. Now, I want to urge you to draw out these qualities from your boy's own reading — and to do it, you have to show an interest in what he is reading and establish a dialogue about it.

'What is that you're reading?' you ask. 'Tell me about it.' (This is not the same as a teacher asking for a book summary.) 'That's interesting. I didn't know that,' you continue. 'You got it from this book did you? Can I have a look? I might borrow that from you when you're finished.'

Do it, too. Read a few pages sometime on your own, then come back to him to discuss it or make further comments. Boys will bend your ear for hours (if you let them) about what they have read, and won't they hurry back to the book to find out more to assail you with! This can happen with both fiction and non-fiction equally. It is the literary equivalent of kicking a ball around in the backyard with your dad.

Involvement and commitment, as the words imply, ask of your time and effort and perseverance. Perseverance and commitment are qualities prized among men. You need to be committed to playing your part as your son learns to read. Households where the child-rearing activities are shared rather than divided between the mother and father are more likely to produce boys who read. Reading to your son is included in this. Listening to him read is vital as well. This is how you help him to reach the level of fluency he needs.

You can get further involved by joining the library yourself and sharing the task of taking your son to change his books. Help him browse to find the best stuff and borrow some books yourself. Look out for material that he would not normally choose, but which you think he will like if you share it with him. If you want your son to connect with novels rather than a diet of magazines and information books, you can help to steer him in that direction. It is through this involvement that fathers and other men in a boy's life can break down the mind set that reading is a feminine thing. Involving yourself from the earliest years and extending that involvement right through your son's schooling will help to stem the drift away from reading that so many boys experience.

Boys and novels

You, better than a boy's mother, appreciate that the pleasure of novels for a lot of males is in what they find out — all manner of geographical and historical trivia that builds their store of general knowledge.

This has certainly been a feature of my reading, and that of many men I know. One of the first adult novels I read for pleasure was Something of Value *by Robert Ruark, set in Kenya during the brutal Mau Mau rebellion. Much as I cared about the lives and loves of the main characters, it was the setting that fascinated me — the hunting, the safaris, farming in Africa, the tribal customs of the Kikuyu. As a matter of fact, the Kikuyu have this amazing way of identifying thieves and liars. They heat up a machete and the suspects have to line up and poke out their — Sorry, I was getting carried away ...*

But you see my point. The novels of James Michener have been a personal favourite for the same reason. I am a history and geography guy. I love maps and majored in history at uni. I have a friend who loves fast cars. It is not surprising that what novels he gets round to reading feature fast cars and the fast life that surrounds them. Neither of us find any appeal in novels so heavily focused on human relationships that they could take place anywhere in the western world.

In late primary and especially into the teenage years, you can be your son's connection to narrative fiction. It may not be through the literary works he is asked to read for school, but through the 'pulp' fiction that is so enjoyable that this connection will be sustained.

The importance of reading books to your son has been covered in chapter seven. It is enough to remind you here that this is a very powerful way to demonstrate what you value and to get involved. You might consider this also. A Canadian study showed that in cases where most of the reading to children was done by fathers, reading was viewed by both boys and girls as an acceptable masculine activity. Another study showed that where fathers took an active role in reading to children and their early literacy development, not only did boys benefit, but girls as well.

Keep this in mind as you consider the stereotyped views which will put pressure on your son. Influential though you are in shaping his attitudes, you are not the only influence. His peer group and the media become increasingly significant as he grows. If, even at an early age, he shows a strong consciousness of his difference from girls and women, then it is up to you to see that he does not associate reading purely with the feminine. Hopefully, a balance between parents will support a gender-neutral view of books and reading. Ultimately, though, the many advantages to be gained from reading to children and being involved in their literacy development are more important than which parent does the reading.

CHAPTER TEN

A note to mothers who have no male partner in the home

All children need role models. To grow up without them would be like sailing the wide oceans alone, without a map, a compass or a star to steer by. Role models are not confined to people of the same sex — boys learn a great deal about how to behave as human beings from their mothers. This is an important point to remember throughout what follows. But, inevitably, a boy must seek models of masculine behaviour to copy, to measure himself against, or simply to reject, in order to establish his identity as a man in the making.

Mothers are aware of this, I am sure. For women who no longer have the father of their sons present in the household, finding suitable role models for boys among the extended family and social network is a vital and at times difficult responsibility. Grandfathers, uncles and older brothers are not always able or willing to play such a role. Other men, even those willing to help, have their own lives and often their own families to consider.

Sporting coaches, scout leaders and the like can become significant in a boy's life, but many men in these positions feel compelled to act out the dominant masculine stereotypes which, as we have seen, can work against good reading habits for boys. Consequently, a woman cannot be sure that such men will support the positive attitudes needed.

The vacuum for growing boys can be filled all too easily with the heroes depicted in films, television programs, video games and other media. While some of these heroes deserve the respect and admiration of boys, it is often the harmful stereotypes that abound — ones in which books and reading are invisible, irrelevant or disdained. Boys without a man close at hand, as an imperfect but warmly human presence, can come to believe that these media images of masculinity are the norm rather than a fantasy. Trying to live up to such impossible ideals can be as harmful to boys as the Barbie doll ideal can be to girls.

The other way that a vacuum of masculine role models becomes filled is through the peer group. Once they start school, boys spend more time with their friends than with adult males. Narrow views of acceptable masculine behaviour can be strictly policed by peers. While it is not unheard of that books and reading can be a focal point for a group of boys, this is rarely the case without sensitive and intelligent intervention from adults. Again, boys without a real man to measure the bravado and exaggeration of their peer group against can form the view that the very act of reading somehow devalues their masculine identity.

What can a mother do? To begin, I would like to suggest a rather startling concept. Some women without a male partner in the household can actually be in a more powerful position to influence their sons' development than many women with male partners. Put bluntly, Dad can be part of the problem — especially if he himself has been brought up to believe that books are for girls and all but functional reading is a waste of time. Indeed, a mother who has carefully nurtured her son's reading habits can see all her work swept away by a single disparaging comment from a father who does not support her efforts. Adult men and a boy's friends are not the only ones who police his performance of masculine roles. Boys are aware that women and girls are watching and judging them too. All boys look to their mothers for confirmation that their behaviour is accepted as masculine, especially boys without fathers in the home. So use this freedom from a potentially negative attitude to raise a son who sees reading as useful and fun for everyone. Help him to build a proud and confident sense of his own masculinity that is separate from the narrow stereotypes so widely presented. As a woman and a mother, think through what kind of man you want your son to become, what you would be proud to see him achieve and picture what place books and reading will take in the life of this man you are helping to create. This is important, because whether you realise it or not, you will pass your hopes and expectations on to him.

As part of this nurturing process, you need to establish reading as a gender-neutral behaviour in your son's mind. To him, reading to you and with you and, later, reading by himself should be something that boys do. Praise him for his reading and link it to his growth towards manhood in the comments you make. A boy who has pride and confidence in his reading will not surrender it easily. Even if he is aware that books do not rate highly with his mates, he will still read happily within the home and when expected to do so in school.

Perhaps I was being rather harsh towards members of my own gender earlier when I hinted that no role model is better than a negative role model (and please realise I was referring only to reading attitudes). In defence of my own gender, it must be noted that fathers no longer living in the home have by no means surrendered an interest in their sons' well-being. Most remain willing to do what they can to see that their boy does well at school and grows towards a richly satisfying adulthood. Support for reading habits and attitudes is part of this, and so should be sought from non-custodial fathers. When a boy goes to spend time with his father, a book should be one of the things he takes along. It may be the book you are currently reading to him, and his father can continue with the next chapter. Fathers should be actively encouraged to give books of their own choosing as presents along with more traditional gifts. One scenario you should be keen to avoid is

where a boy perceives his father's house to be a place without books. He might need to have a store of his own books that 'live' permanently in his father's home, though this would work better if his father is seen to have some ownership of this stockpile by adding to it and selecting books for shared reading from it.

There will be men who become significant in your boy's life at various stages — grandfathers, uncles, teachers and coaches. Where you feel comfortable in doing so, you should approach these men and ask them to support your son's reading habits by:

- occasionally taking the opportunity to talk to him about his reading;
- showing approval of and interest in his reading;

- mentioning, with enthusiasm, the books they read as boys — even lending books to the boy as a special consideration (a coach can lend a book of coaching hints, a biography of a great player, or even a novel set against the background of a sport); and
- showing themselves to be proudly masculine readers.

The male teachers encountered by your son have the potential to influence him very strongly. I have said already in this book that I view it as a fundamental responsibility for male teachers to model positive reading attitudes in schools. For boys who have no adult male in the household this becomes even more important. Sometimes, such men need to be made aware of this responsibility — just a gentle nudge, perhaps a quiet word at a parent-teacher interview, can make all the difference. Others are terrific without any prompting, such as the Year 3 teacher I met in Perth who has his pupils, boys as much as girls, besotted with poetry.

At home, you will be the one who reads to your son and helps him through the learning-to-read stage, as most other mothers do. Be sure to encourage him to use books and reading to explore his boyishness. This will help him to separate his reading behaviour from any perceptions that it is a female pursuit, concerned only with female interests and themes. Your support for boyishness will be proven through the books and magazines you encourage him to choose from bookshops, newsagencies and libraries, all of which will add to his ownership of reading. If some of these seem strongly devoted to masculine stereotypes, remember that the books you read to him will provide a range of positive masculine models, from tales of traditional heroes to more thoughtful stories about boys dealing with friendship or death or alienation or handling life in a single-parent home.

All of this discussion has centred on building and supporting positive attitudes. Other strategies mentioned in earlier chapters, such as establishing a place to read and a time to read, and providing a household with plenty of reading material available, apply in the same way they do in any home. These strategies, combined with efforts to engender positive attitudes, will give a boy lacking a father's example close at hand every chance to grow up within a culture of reading.

Books for boys

List 1

The early years

The following books are for babies and preschoolers. They are bright, colourful and rhythmic, can be re-read many times, and are great for talking about, predicting and recounting.

Eric Carle
  The Very Hungry Caterpillar
Pamela Allen
  Who Sank the Boat?; the *Mr McGee* books; *I Wish I
  Had a Pirate Suit; Bertie and the Bear*
Colin and Jacqui Hawkins
  Tog the Dog; Mig the Pig
Pat Hutchins
  Rosie's Walk; Don't Forget the Bacon!
Janet and Allan Ahlberg
  The Baby's Catalogue; Peepo!; Each Peach Pear Plum
Rod Campbell
  Dear Zoo; Oh Dear!
Martin Waddell
  Owl Babies; Can't You Sleep, Little Bear?
Helen Oxenbury
  Tickle, Tickle; All Fall Down
Alison Lester
  Magic Beach
Michael Rosen
  We're Going on a Bear Hunt

Cathy Wilcox
  Enzo the Wonderfish
Gene Zion
  Harry the Dirty Dog
Lynley Dodd
  Hairy Maclary from Donaldson's Dairy
Maurice Sendak
  Where the Wild Things Are

List 2

Preschoolers and the first years at school

The titles listed here are picture storybooks for children from preschool through to the first three years at school. Some are quite long, and many have a more complicated or mature storyline than the books recommended in List 1.

Anthony Browne
  Willy the Wimp; Willy the Champ
Terry Denton
  Felix and Alexander
Judith Viorst
  Alexander and the Terrible, Horrible, No Good, Very Bad Day
Janet and Andrew McLean
  Josh
Rod Clement
  Just Another Ordinary Day; Counting on Frank

Margaret Wild
  Tom Goes to Kindergarten; There's a Sea in My Bedroom
Virginia Lee Burton
  Mike Mulligan and His Steam Shovel
Dr Seuss
  The Sneetches and Other Stories; If I Ran the Circus;
  The Cat in the Hat
Anna Fienberg
  The Hottest Boy Who Ever Lived
Tomi Ungerer
  The Beast of Monsieur Racine; The Hat;
  The Three Robbers
Janell Cannon
  Stellaluna
Shirley Hughes
  Dogger; Alfie Gets in First
Mem Fox
  Wombat Divine
John Burningham
  Mr Gumpy's Motor Car; Come Away From
  the Water Shirley
Robert N. Munsch
  The Paper Bag Princess
Jenny Wagner
  John Brown, Rose and the Midnight Cat; Aranea
Babette Cole
  Princess Smartypants
Roald Dahl
  The Giraffe and the Pelly and Me; The Enormous
  Crocodile; Revolting Rhymes; Dirty Beasts

Bob Graham
  Rose Meets Mr Wintergarten; Crusher is Coming;
  Greetings from Sandy Beach
Gillian Rubinstein
  Sharon, Keep Your Hair On
Bruce Whatley
  Looking for Crabs; Detective Donut and the
  Wild Goose Chase
Allan Baillie
  Dragon Quest
Graeme Base
  The Sign of the Seahorse; Animalia

List 3

Chapter books for reading aloud

This list suggests books for reading aloud by parents (a chapter or two each night) when children need to stretch beyond the picture book. (The picture book read in one sitting should not suddenly disappear — a gradual change is recommended.)

The need for chapter books grows about the time a child starts school, though there are no hard and fast rules. Some children will listen as books are being read to older brothers and sisters from as young as three years old. This list should satisfy up to the age of nine or ten. Again, no definite cut-off age can be set. List 7 carries on from here with suggestions for later primary and lower secondary age groups.

Randolph Stow
  Midnite
E.B. White
  Charlotte's Web
C.S. Lewis
  The Lion, the Witch and the Wardrobe
Colin Thiele
  Storm Boy
James Roy
  Captain Mack
Beverley Cleary
  Ramona Quimby, Age 8 (or any *Ramona* book)
Russell Hoban
  The Mouse and His Child
Odo Hirsch
  Antonio S and the Mystery of Theodore Guzman
Robin Klein
  Hating Alison Ashley
Anna Fienberg
  The Magnificent Nose and Other Marvels
Lynne Reid Banks
  The Indian in the Cupboard (and other books in the series)
Robert O'Brien
  Mrs Frisby and the Rats of NIMH; The Silver Crown
Ted Hughes
  The Iron Man
Margery Williams
  The Velveteen Rabbit

List 4

Newly independent readers

Once a boy can read by himself, he needs these books to enjoy on his own. Some can be read in one sitting. Those that take a little longer have short chapters. This list will help the average reader through Years 3, 4 and into Year 5, where the more demanding books of List 5 should gradually take over.

Kate Walker
   I Hate Books!
Leigh Hobbs
   Old Tom; Old Tom's Guide to Being Good
Kim Caraher
   The Cockroach Cup
Annette Butterworth
   Jake in Danger
Gary Paulsen
   Gary Paulsen's World of Adventure series
Emily Rodda
   Bob the Builder and the Elves
Terry Deary
   Horrible Histories:
   The Terrible Tudors
   The Awesome Egyptians
   The Angry Aztecs

Aussie Bites series (various authors)
    Fort Island (David Metzenthen)
    The Horrible Holiday (Catherine Jinks)
    Down in the Dump with Dinsmore (Margaret Mahy)
    No Place for Grubbs (Max Dann)
Morris Lurie
    The 27th Annual African Hippopotamus Race
Gillian Rubinstein
    Jake and Pete (and other *Jake and Pete* stories)
Max Dann
    Adventures With My Worst Best Friend (and sequels)
Jeff Brown
    Flat Stanley
Robin Klein
    Thing; Thingnapped!
Michaela Morgan
    Sick as a Parrot
Elizabeth Laird
    Stinker Muggles and the Dazzle Bug
Colin and Jacqui Hawkins
    Pirates
Margaret Mahy
    The Dentist's Promise
Wendy Orr
    Paradise Palace
Dianne Bates
    Grandma Cadbury's Trucking Tales
Brian Caswell
    Relax Max!

Duncan Ball
  Emily Eyefinger (and series)
Arnold Sobol
  Encyclopedia Brown (and series)
Osmar White
  The Superoo of Mungalongaloo
Jon Scieszka
  The Stinky Cheese Man and Other Fairly Stupid Tales;
  The Time Warp Trio; The True Story of the Three Little
  Pigs; The Frog Prince Continued; Squids Will Be Squids
Tadpole series
  Hero (Sally Odgers)
  Sir Joshua and the Unprofessional
  Dragon (Sam Bowring)
  Blackbread the Pirate (Garth Nix)
  Bill the Inventor (Garth Nix)
Moya Simons
  Totally Cool!; Totally Weird!; Totally Awesome!;
  Totally Freaky!
Peter McFarlane
  Bruce the Goose; Barnaby the Barbarian
Janeen Brian
  Dog Star
Phil Cummings
  The Great Jimbo James

List 5

Middle and upper primary

Boys as young as Year 4 will enjoy these. By Year 5, boys keen to use their reading skills to enjoy longer and more mature stories will find plenty here. A range of tastes are catered for — everything from the weird and wacky to the deeply moving.

Emily Rodda
  Rowan of Rin (and series)
J.K. Rowling
  The *Harry Potter* series
Bob Cattell
  The *Glory Gardens* series
Duncan Ball
  The *Selby* series
Judy Blume
  Tales of a Fourth Grade Nothing
Margaret Clark
  Hold My Hand or Else (and many others)
Gillian Cross
  The Demon Headmaster
Colin Dann
  The Animals of Farthing Wood (and series)
Hunter Davies
  Snotty Bumstead
Sid Fleischman
  McBroom's Wonderful One Acre Farm

C.S. Lewis
> *The Lion, the Witch and the Wardrobe*

David Caddy
> *Smash Whammy!*

James Moloney
> *Swashbuckler; Buzzard Breath and Brains*

Moya Simons
> *Dead Average!; Dead Meat!*

Michael Stephens
> *Eddie the Great; Ghost Train; Titans!*

Paul Stafford
> *Ned Kelly's Helmet; Blatantly Bogus; Basically Bollocks*

Sports Max series (various authors)
> *Kick Back* (David Hill)
> *Seconds Best* (David Hill)
> *Fat, Four-eyed and Useless* (David Hill)

Elaine Forrestal
> *Graffiti on the Fence*

David Metzenthen
> *Brocky's Bananagram*

Anthony Horowitz
> *The Devil and His Boy*

Dav Pilkey
> *The Adventures of Captain Underpants*

Jacqueline Wilson
> *Cliffhanger*

Elizabeth Honey
> *Don't Pat the Wombat!*

Simon French
> *Cannily, Cannily*

Jenny Pausacker
 Fast Forward
Warren Flynn
 Gaz (and sequels)
Wendy Jenkins
 Killer Boots
Wendy Orr
 Dirtbikes
Gareth Owen
 The Final Test
Roy Pond
 Knight School; The Mummy Monster Game
Philip Ridley
 Meteorite Spoon
Colin Thompson
 Attila the Bluebottle
Christobel Mattingley
 No Gun for Asmir
Allan Baillie
 Little Brother
Arthur Roth
 Iceberg Hermit
Lois Lowry
 The Giver
Terry Pratchett
 Truckers; Johnny and the Dead; the *Discworld* series
Morris Gleitzman
 Two Weeks With the Queen

Gary Paulsen
  Mr Tucket; Tucket's Ride; A Soldier's Heart;
  Hatchet (and series)
Brian Jacques
  Redwall (and series)
Colin Bowles
  Surfing Mr Petrovic
J. Eldridge
  Behind Enemy Lines
John Larkin
  Ghost Byte; Spaghetti Legs; Growing Payne;
  the *Western Wildcats* series
Michael de Larrabeiti
  The Borribles (and series)
Catherine Jinks
  Pagan's Crusade (and series); *The Stinking Great Lie*
Margaret Clark
  Footy Shorts; Board Shorts (and others in the series)
John Marsden
  Looking for Trouble; Staying Alive in Year Five;
  Creep Street
Rory Barnes
  Horsehead Boy; Horsehead Man
Bryce Courtenay
  The Power of One: Young Readers' Edition
Add to these the comic-style stories featuring Asterix
(by Goscinny and Uderzo) and TinTin (by Hergè).

List 6

Picture books for older readers

In recent years, the power of illustration has been harnessed to tell stories not just for the very young, but for children of upper primary age and older. Boys love them.

Gary Crew
  The Watertower; The Viewer
Paul Jennings
  Grandad's Gifts; Duck for Cover; Spooner or Later
Elizabeth Stanley
  The Deliverance of Dancing Bears
Libby Hathorn
  Way Home
Anthony Browne
  King Kong
Margaret Barbalet
  The Wolf
Raymond Briggs
  Fungus the Bogeyman; Father Christmas
Michael Foreman
  After the War Was Over
Peter Collington
  The Coming of Surfman

List 7

Reading aloud into upper primary and early secondary

This list suggests titles for reading aloud to boys ranging in age from ten to thirteen. Boys are stepping out, learning more of the world, but also becoming aware of how cruel it can be at times. They expect this experience to be reflected in what is read to them. Unfortunately, it is impossible to judge the interests and sensitivities of all boys in this range. With this in mind, I have graduated the list, so that books which would suit the older end of the age group are found towards the bottom of the list.

Betsy Byars
The Eighteenth Emergency
James Moloney
Swashbuckler; Buzzard Breath and Brains
Beverley Cleary
Dear Mr Henshaw
Jean George
My Side of the Mountain; Julie of the Wolves
Katherine Paterson
Bridge to Terabithia
Michelle Magorian
Goodnight Mister Tom
Marion D. Bauer
On My Honor

Alan Garner
  The Weirdstone of Brisingamen
Colin Thiele
  The Fire in the Stone
Victor Kelleher
  Master of the Grove
Ann Holm
  I Am David
Ian Serraillier
  The Silver Sword
Lois Lowry
  The Giver
Thurley Fowler
  The Green Wind
Meindert De Jong
  Hurry Home Candy; The House of Sixty Fathers
Theodore Taylor
  The Cay
John Christopher
  White Mountains
E.L.Konigsburg
  The View From Saturday
Katherine Paterson
  The Great Gilly Hopkins
Caroline Macdonald
  The Lake at the End of the World
Roger Vaughan Carr
  Firestorm!
Margaret Mahy
  The Haunting

Jack London
   White Fang
Pat Moon
   The Spying Game
James Houston
   Frozen Fire: A tale of courage
Robert Newton Peck
   A Day No Pigs Would Die
Victor Canning
   The Runaways
Robert Westall
   The Machine Gunners
David Almond
   Kit's Wilderness

List 8

Early and mid-secondary

John Marsden
   Tomorrow When the War Began and series;
   The Great Gatenby; Checkers
Tim Winton
   The Lockie Leonard trilogy
Pat Moon
   The Spying Game
Gary Paulsen
   Canyons; The Voyage of the Frog; A Soldier's Heart

Philip Pullman
  Northern Lights (*His Dark Materials* series)
Ben Bo
  XTREME series: *Skull Crack; The Edge*
Isobelle Carmody
  The Gathering
Judith Clarke
  The Lost Day
Brian Caswell
  A Cage of Butterflies
S.E. Hinton
  The Outsiders; Tex; Taming the Star Runner
Steven Herrick
  Love, Ghosts and Nose Hair; A Place Like This
Libby Hathorn
  Rift
Phillip Gwynne
  Deadly Unna?
Victor Kelleher
  Taronga; The Hunting of Shadroth; The Red King
Lee-Anne Levy
  Jake
Robert Swindells
  Stone Cold
David Metzenthen
  Johnny Hart's Heroes; Falling Forward; Roadie
J.R.R. Tolkien
  The Hobbit
James Moloney
  Dougy; A Bridge to Wiseman's Cove; Crossfire

Gillian Cross
  Wolf
Robin Klein and Max Dann
  The Lonely Hearts Club
Gillian Rubinstein
  Galax Arena; Space Demons (and sequels)
Matt Zurbo
  Idiot Pride
Maureen McCarthy
  Ganglands
David Harris
  The *Cliffhangers* series
Peter McFarlane
  The Enemy You Killed
Ken Catran
  Running Dogs
Anne Fine
  Flour Babies; The Book of the Banshee
Terry Pratchett
  Truckers; Johnny and the Dead; the *Discworld* series
Scott Monk
  Boyz 'R' Us; Raw
Robert Westall
  The Stones of Muncaster Cathedral; Gulf
Shorts series
  The Last Shot (Allan Baillie)
  Graffiti Dog (Eleanor Nilsson)
Nick Earls
  After January

Chris Wheat
  Loose Lips
Archimede Fusillo
  Sparring With Shadows
Robert Cormier
  The Chocolate War; I Am the Cheese
Anne Provoost
  Falling
Anonymous
  Go Ask Alice
Melvin Burgess
  Junk
Laurie Stiller
  Packing It
Simon Higgins
  Beyond the Shaking Time

List 9

Adult books with appeal for boys

Baroness Orczy
  The Scarlet Pimpernel
Arthur Conan Doyle
  The Adventures of Sherlock Holmes
Edgar Allan Poe
  Murders in the Rue Morgue
C.S. Forester
  The Young Hornblower

Dick Francis
For Kicks; Bonecrack (and many more)

Ellis Peters
A Morbid Taste for Bones (the *Brother Cadfael* series)

Agatha Christie
And Then There Were None (and many others)

Frederick Forsyth
The Day of the Jackal; The Fourth Protocol;
The Odessa File

Carl Sagan
Contact

Len Deighton
The Ipcress File; Game, Set and Match

Jack Higgins
The Eagle Has Landed

Alistair MacLean
The Guns of Navarone

James Michener
Texas; Space; Chesapeake

James Herriot
All Creatures Great and Small

Sue Grafton
A is for Alibi (and many more)

Robert Harris
Fatherland; Enigma

Bryce Courtenay
The Power of One

Lorenzo Carcaterra
Sleepers

Jeffrey Archer
   *Kane and Abel; A Matter of Honour; Not a Penny
   More, Not a Penny Less; A Quiver Full of Arrows;
   A Twist in the Tale*
Stephen King
   The Tommyknockers; Christine; Dark Visions
John Grisham
   The Firm; The Chamber; The Client
Tom Clancy
   The Hunt for Red October; Clear and Present Danger
Michael Crichton
   The Andromeda Strain; Congo; Jurassic Park
Wilbur Smith
   *When the Lion Feeds; The Sound of Thunder;
   The Sunbird*
Patricia Cornwell
   Body of Evidence (the Kay Scarpetta series)
Bernard Cornwell
   Rebel
Henri Charriere
   Papillon
Clive Cussler
   Raise the Titanic
Nick Earls
   Zigzag Street
Ken Follett
   On Wings of Eagles
Robert Ludlum
   The Bourne Supremacy; The Matarese Circle

Ruth Rendell
  the Inspector Wexford series
Colin Dexter
  the Inspector Morse series
Ernest Hemingway
  Death in the Afternoon
Jack Kerouac
  On the Road
George Orwell
  Animal Farm
William Golding
  Lord of the Flies
Tom Wolfe
  The Right Stuff

List 10

Sure-fire winners

These are books that shouldn't be read to boys — because they will happily read them on their own. Two names dominate here: Paul Jennings and Roald Dahl. As far as I am concerned, they both deserve the Nobel Prize for (getting boys into) Literature. John Marsden is not far behind with his War series for boys aged twelve and up.

For newly independent readers, Dahl's titles include *Fantastic Mr Fox*, *George's Marvellous Medicine*, *The Twits*, *Esio Trot* and *The Vicar of Nibbleswicke*. His middle and upper primary titles include *Charlie and the*

Chocolate Factory, James and the Giant Peach, Danny the Champion of the World, The Witches (my favourite), The BFG, Matilda and the autobiographies, Boy and Going Solo. The latter two titles you might decide to read to your son after all. Boy, in particular, is too good to miss.

Paul Jennings has two fantastic illustrated books created in conjunction with Ted Greenwood and Terry Denton — Spooner or Later and Duck for Cover. After these, The Cabbage Patch Fib and The Paw Thing suit boys just coming out of the newly independent stage. Both have spawned many sequels, as has The Gizmo, which should follow. For middle and upper primary boys, his classic Un series is perfect. These are collections of stories, and titles include: Unreal, Uncovered, Unbelievable and Unmentionable, plus Quirky Tales and Round the Twist, which is related to the TV series. Avoid introducing these collections too early as the humour and quirkiness can go over the head of seven and eight year olds. Some of the stories are quite dark as well, though still highly entertaining. If a reluctant male reader managed to make it to high school without being offered a Paul Jennings book (though this is unlikely), then make his day.

Books noted on the rest of this list have appeared in previous lists but gain a second mention here as 'sure-fire' winners. The Harry Potter books listed are rapidly surpassing the legendary status of Dahl and Jennings. The list is ordered so that books for older boys appear towards the end.

Morris Lurie
  The 27th Annual African Hippopotamus Race
Tim Winton
  The Bugalugs Bum Thief
Andy Griffiths
  Just Tricking; Just Annoying
Arnold Sobol
  Encyclopedia Brown (and series)
Osmar White
  The Superoo of Mungalongaloo
Judy Blume
  Tales of a Fourth Grade Nothing; Superfudge
Bruce Coville
  My Teacher Flunked the Planet
Thomas Rockwell
  How to Eat Fried Worms
Barbara Robinson
  The Worst Kids in the World
Rachel Flynn
  I Hate Fridays
J.K. Rowling
  the Harry Potter series
Gary Crew
  The Watertower (a picture book for older readers)
Morris Gleitzman
  Misery Guts; Worry Warts; Blabbermouth; Toad Rage
Louis Sachar
  Holes
Terry Pratchett
  Truckers; Johnny and the Dead; the *Discworld* series

Tim Winton
  Lockie Leonard Human Torpedo
Gary Paulsen
  Hatchet
David McRobbie
  The Wayne Dynasty
John Marsden
  Tomorrow When the War Began (and series)
Gillian Rubinstein
  Space Demons
James Moloney
  Crossfire; A Bridge to Wiseman's Cove
Sue Townsend
  The Secret Diary of Adrian Mole Aged 13¾

List 11

Series books

After Dark
  an Australian series of short illustrated stories with
  ghostly or terrifying happenings; authors include
  Gary Crew, Carmel Bird, James Moloney, Garry
  Disher and Isobelle Carmody
Animorphs
  a sci-fi series linked to a TV series

Strange Matter
   a horror series by various authors
Creepers
   a horror series by Bill Condon and Robert Hood
Spinechillers
   a horror series by various authors
Hardy Boys
   a longstanding American mystery/adventure series
Crimebusters
   formerly known as The Three Investigators; another
   longstanding American mystery/adventure series
The X Files
   horror series linked to the TV series
Clue
   a mystery series related to the board game Cluedo
Willard Price adventure series
   non-stop action; titles include *Lion Adventure* and
   Arctic Adventure
Goosebumps
   phenomenally popular horror series which became
   a TV series
Star Wars
   junior novelisations from the films
Star Trek
   a series related to the popular TV series

List 12

Strictly non-fiction

Non-fiction for boys in upper primary and lower secondary.

The Guinness Book of Records

Jennifer Beck, Dyan Blacklock and Katrina Allan

Crash! The Search for the Stinson

Terry Deary

Horrible Histories (see List 4); *Horrible Geographies*

Dexter Planet

A Boy's Guide to Life

Bill Scheller

Spaced Out

True Stories series (various authors)

Stoked! (Glyn Parry)

Bog Bodies (Natalie Jane Prior)

Mysterious Ruins (Prior)

Plague and Pestilence (Magrete Lamond)

Incredible Journeys (Rick Wilkinson)

Caves, Graves and Catacombs (Natalie Jane Prior)

Soccer (Damien Lovelock)

Rock Raps (Meredith Costain)

B. Guthridge

Travelling Solo to Japan; Travelling Solo to Morocco

Oxford Children's Pocket Book of Facts

Jean Marzollo

I Spy series

David Harris and Max Jones
  A Man Called Possum
Mike Lefroy
  Shipwreck at Madman's Corner
various authors
  Dorling Kindersley's *Eyewitness Guides*
Stephen Biesty
  Cross-Sections series
A.B. Facey
  A Fortunate Life (abridged version)
Dava Sobel
  Longitude
Rod Tokely and Dillon Naylor
  Zap! Splat! Ka-pow! Make Your Own Comic
Karl Kruszelnicki
  Great Australian Facts & Firsts series
  Flight, Food & Thingummyjigs
  Ears, Gears & Gadgets
  Forests, Fleece & Prickly Pears
Paul Holper and Simon Torok
  Wow! Amazing Science Facts and Trivia

List 13

Poetry

A boy's wary attitude towards poetry will quickly change once he reads (or hears) poems from these collections.

Elizabeth Honey
  Mongrel Doggerel; Honey Sandwich
Roald Dahl
  Dirty Beasts; Roald Dahl's Revolting Rhymes
Michael Rosen
  Tea in the Sugar Bowl, Potato in My Shoe
Steven Herrick
  Waterbombs
Gary Crew
  Troy Thompson's Excellent Peotry Book
Colin McNaughton
  There's an Awful Lot of Weirdos in Our Neighbourhood;
  Who's Been Sleeping in My Porridge?;
  Making Friends with Frankenstein
Komninos
  The Baby Rap and Other Poems
June Factor
  Far Out, Brussel Sprout!; Unreal, Banana Peel!;
  All right, Vegemite!; Real Keen, Baked Bean!
Peter Durkin
  You Beaut, Juicy Fruit!
Tomi Ungerer
  Oh, That's Ridiculous!

Doug MacLeod
  Sister Madge's Book of Nuns
Tony Bradman
  Our Side of the Playground: What Boys Think of Girls
Shel Silverstein
  Falling Up
Colin Thompson
  The Dog's Just Been Sick in the Honda and Other Poems
Wallace Tripp
  A Great Big Ugly Man Came Up and Tied His Horse to Me: A book of nonsense verse

List 14

Funny books

Librarians cringe when boys ask for something funny. 'I want something that will make me laugh,' say the boys. Yet humour is such a personal thing; what will have one boy rolling about in fits of laughter will leave another cold. If a boy just wants to be assured of laughing out loud two or three times on every page, then maybe he should try one of the many joke books available. In the context of a story, though, the best an author can do is write with a sense of fun. All of the following books do this. They have been ordered so that the more challenging humour for boys going into secondary school is placed towards the end.

Andy Griffiths
Just Tricking; Just Stupid; Just Annoying
Paul Stafford
Basically Bollocks; Blatantly Bogus; Ned Kelly's Helmet
Doug MacLeod
Frank Boulderbuster
Morris Gleitzman
Misery Guts (and sequels); *Blabbermouth* (and
sequels); *Toad Rage* and many more
David Metzenthen
Brocky's Bananagram
Barbara Robinson
The Worst Kids in the World
Anthony Horowitz
*Groosham Grange; Granny; The Falcon's Malteser;
Public Enemy Number Two; South by South-East*
Geoffrey McSkimming
The Cairo Jim series
David McRobbie
The Wayne Dynasty (and sequels)
Gary Paulsen
Harris and Me
Tim Winton
Lockie Leonard Human Torpedo (and sequels)
Linda Aronson
*Kelp: A Tale of First Love, Seaweed and
Rupert Murdoch; Rude Health*
Judith Clarke
The Heroic Life of Al Capsella

John Marsden
  The Great Gatenby
Jocelyn Harewood
  Voices in the Wash-house

List 15

Fantasy

Some wonderful fantasy has been written especially for young readers. The first list names some of the best. However, these titles can be seen as 'worthy' by boys, particularly when they reach high school. The second list contains fantasy for a more general readership, and these books may hold more appeal for such readers.

List 1

Isobelle Carmody: *Obernewtyn*
Susan Cooper: *Over Sea, Under Stone* (and the rest
    of the Dark is Rising series)
C.S. Lewis: *The Lion, the Witch and the Wardrobe*
    (the Chronicles of Narnia)
Ursula Le Guin: *A Wizard of Earthsea*
Garth Nix: *Sabriel*
Philip Pullman: *Northern Lights*
J.R.R. Tolkien: *The Hobbit*
Jane Yolen: *Dragon's Blood*
Lloyd Alexander: *The Book of Three* (Chronicles
    of Prydain)
Tamora Pierce: *Wild Magic*

List 2

Terry Brooks: *The Sword of Shannara* (and series)
Sara Douglass: the Battleaxe trilogy
David Eddings: *Pawn of Prophecy* (the Belgariad series)
Raymond E. Feist: *Magician*
Guy Gavriel Kay: *The Summer Tree*
J.R.R. Tolkien: *The Lord of the Rings*
Stephen Donaldson: *Lord Foul's Bane*
David Gemmell: *Bloodstone; Druss the Legend*
Stephen Lawhead: *The Black Rood; The Iron Lance*
Tad Williams: *The Dragonbone Chair; Caliban's Hour*